Praise for *What You Don't Know and Your Boss Won't Tell You*

"A terrific combination of strategy and in-the-trenches tactical counsel that will benefit any young woman (or man!) entering the workforce. Packed with several lifetimes' worth of lessons from the front lines, this book provides insight and offers practical solutions to almost any situation you can encounter as you build your career."

—**Shoba Purushothaman**, Chief Executive Officer,
The NewsMarket, New York, NY

"This is an invaluable resource for those who want to succeed the smart way. Lenehan packs the book with commonsense, practical success tips. I wish this book had been available to me early in my career."

—**Patricia M. Annino**, Partner, Prince Lobel Glovsky and Tye LLP,
author of *Women & Money*, Boston, MA

"Every career-hopeful young person needs a mentor; this book provides 35 of them. The wealth of practical advice can also benefit people at every stage of their career."

—**Ilene B. Jacobs**, retired Executive Vice President, Human Resources,
Fidelity Investments; former Senior Vice President, Human Resources,
Digital Equipment Corporation, Boston, MA

"For bosses and managers, this book should be required reading! For young professionals learning to navigate their corporate careers, this is a wise and positive book full of commonsense advice."

—**Kevin P. Newman**, President, Kevin P. Newman Associates;
former President of Atlantic Pacific Capital;
former Managing Director at Lehman Brothers,
Trust Company of the West, and CS First Boston, Darien, CT

"Every working woman—regardless of what stage in her career she is in—should keep this book by her bedside for frequent reference. This book is filled with invaluable pointers that no one ever says out loud. Learning the ropes is crucial to corporate success for any woman in industry."

—**Alexandra Pruner**, Senior Vice President,
Gulf Publishing Company, Houston, TX

"If there is only one book you can read about success in your early career . . . this is it! I wish this book was available when I started out in business. It would have saved me from many 'faux pas' and embarrassing moments, and might have provided me with the direction I was looking for. I particularly love the layout of the book that offers quick quips on the dos and don'ts of operating successfully in the business world."

—**Pat Obuchowski**, CEO (Chief Empowerment Officer),
inVisionaria, Foster City, CA

What You Don't Know and Your Boss Won't Tell You

What You Don't Know

▪ and ▪

Your Boss Won't Tell You

✔ *Advice from Senior Female Executives on*
What You Need to Succeed

Pamela F. Lenehan

SYREN BOOK COMPANY
Minneapolis

Most Syren Books are available at special quantity discounts for bulk purchases for sales promotions, premiums, fund-raising, and educational needs. For details, write

Syren Book Company
Special Sales Department
5120 Cedar Lake Road
Minneapolis, MN 55416

Published by
Syren Book Company
5120 Cedar Lake Road
Minneapolis, MN 55416

Printed in the United States of America on acid-free paper

ISBN-13: 978-0-929636-59-7
ISBN-10: 0-929636-59-7

LCCN 2005937697

Cover design by Kyle Hunter
Book design by Rachel Holscher

To order additional copies of this book see the form
at the back of this book or go to www.itascabooks.com

▪ Contents

▪ Preface

When I started my first job in the management training program at a major bank in New York City more than 30 years ago, I was truly a blank slate as far as business was concerned. I had gone to Brown University, a liberal arts college, and grown up with a father who was a doctor and a mother who was an actress, neither of whom knew anything about business. Early in my career I envied those polished young men (they were mostly men) who always seemed to know what to what to say, what to do, and what to wear. With great training, hard work, and a lot of trial and error, I progressed in my career through multiple companies, but I continued to feel that there must be a better way for those of us not born into business families to get the information we needed to succeed.

Approximately 15 years ago, when I moved to Boston from New York, I started getting businesswomen together four or five times a year in the evening for what today is known as networking. One of the recurring conversations over the years was that women were not progressing at the speed we had hoped. We thought more women would be in senior management, especially now that more women were in the pipeline. However, even some of our own daughters, who had benefited from our counsel, struggled. What could we do to give them more specific advice? What exactly did they need to know? From these and other conversations came the idea to write this book. The first step was to generate the list of issues young people in business need to consider, and the second step was to decide which executives to interview. The problem was not that I did not know many great women, the problem was I knew too many, so I had to narrow the list to be sure there was a broad representation of industries, areas of the country, and ethnic backgrounds. I am grateful to all the women I know who were inspirations for this book and who introduced me to many of the people I interviewed.

I would like to thank the 35 women who shared their careers, personal lives, and time with me to answer the long list of questions put to them. More about these women and their backgrounds is covered in the first chapter. A few women cannot be thanked by name owing to company policy or professional concerns. You know who you are, and I have expressed my appreciation privately. The women who have allowed me to thank them publicly are Kathleen Allen, Patricia Baker, Beth Bronner, Margaret Brown, Susan Buffam, Barbara Byrne, Ruby Chandy, Christine Cournoyer, Janet Dunlap, Susan Farrell, Patricia Foye, Marianne Geuss, Lesley Goldwasser, Lee Hanson, Laura Hodges-Taylor, Susan Hunt Stevens, Barbara Jeremiah, Suzanne Nora Johnson, Mary Mattson Kenworthy, Kristine Langdon, Mela Lew, Gail Long, Alicia Lopez, Deborah Lovich, Gail Maderis, Sandra Moose, Kathryn Murphy, Virginia Ruesterholz, Martha Samuelson, Denise Warren, and Phyllis Yale. A lawyer in the group reminded me to say that the views expressed in this book are solely those of the individuals and do not necessarily reflect the opinions of their employers.

I would especially like to thank Sarah and Paul Lenehan, the next generation of the family who have opted for careers in business, for their perspectives, critical comments, and encouragement. To my husband, Larry Geuss, a special thank-you for all the time you spent alone with the dogs while I was working on this book.

What You Don't Know and Your Boss Won't Tell You

One

Why You Don't Know What You Don't Know

The complaints of "He doesn't fit in" or "She just doesn't get it" are common. So why don't managers just tell people what needs to be improved or how to fit in? Managers spend a significant amount of their time on personnel issues, but many think it is an annoyance and that managing people detracts from getting "real" work done.

Most bosses are very comfortable analyzing the performance of a business unit or critiquing a presentation. Few are willing to tackle the complex social issues that are critical for one of their colleagues to be successful in the organization. Sometimes managers are not people-oriented and learned these lessons through trial and error themselves, so they have a hard time articulating their thoughts. Others may not want to hurt people's feelings, especially when some of the comments touch on someone's personality or dress. Finally, in our litigious society many managers simply will not risk hurting their company or career by saying things that are politically incorrect, even if that view is being used to judge performance.

If you plan to move ahead in your career, you need to know about many issues that are not taught in school or discussed in the company handbook. The title *What You Don't Know and Your Boss Won't Tell You* highlights the hard fact that the two people who should be interested in your career—you and your boss—won't have an open dialogue about many issues you need to understand. If you are unlucky enough to have a boss who is not interested in your career, then you especially need this book.

The chapters in this book cover key areas that you need to master. You may already be good at some and need improvement in others. The topics addressed are:

- Actively managing your career on a regular basis
- Learning how to communicate in the language of business

- Effectively using your time while networking and on task forces
- Finding leadership opportunities and good mentors
- Developing a personal style that projects confidence and competence to your boss, clients, and colleagues
- Handling the nuances of dating, emotions, and office politics
- Creating an appearance that will help you succeed
- Understanding the rigors and rules of business travel
- Balancing work and family comfortably

This book is not an exhaustive analysis of each of these subjects, so consider this an executive summary. There are many good business books out there that go into great detail on individual topics. However, this is a book that is meant to be easy to read and cover a lot of ground quickly before you fall into bed exhausted at night after work. At the end of each section within the chapters are take-aways, and at the end of each chapter there is a short list of career-enhancing moves and career-limiting moves.

I have more than 30 years of business experience, including being a partner in a major investment bank and an officer of a public company, but to broaden the perspective I interviewed 35 senior women. They are partners in law, investment banking, consulting, and accounting firms, as well as women at vice president or higher levels in media, technology, biotechnology, and manufacturing firms. I also talked with some younger people to be sure their concerns were addressed. Why just senior women and not men? This started out as a book for younger women, but most of the issues are gender neutral. That makes sense since companies are not looking for a good "female" or "male" employee—they just want an effective employee.

While these women are very senior now, they all started at the bottom and worked their way up. They were not hired out of school as partners of their firms or presidents of their divisions. Collectively, these 35 women and I have worked at more than 100 firms. In addition, they have all managed large groups of people and regularly hired, promoted, and compensated people. These are the type of people you need to understand and impress in order to move up in your organization. Their comments are in quotation marks to set them apart from my introduction of the subjects, although a few of my own experiences are in quotes as well. For convenience, the words *he* and *she* are interchanged rather than writing "he or she" every time.

The women who contributed to this book did so anonymously. They all work for companies with rules regarding what can and cannot be said publicly. The only way to get their honest, unedited responses to the questions, especially the ones that are not politically correct, was to do this on a not-for-attribution basis. For this same reason, not all of the women are even acknowledged in the preface.

What are the executives like? They are married, divorced, and single, with and without children, from different educational and ethnic backgrounds and areas of the country. They were chosen for their diversity, defined very broadly. I met with each woman separately to be sure there was no tendency for someone to soften comments as a result of being in a group. Where there were differences of opinions on the subjects, I have tried to indicate the majority opinion while giving voice to the outliers, since the unusual advice may be useful to some readers and intriguing at the very least.

The contributors rearranged their calendars and often met under stressful situations. One person had just been promoted to head of her region and told her assistant to hold all the congratulatory calls until we finished. One woman's nanny had just quit, and she was taking calls from employment agencies between questions. Another was in the political battle of her life, which I did not know until I heard about it later. Why were these women so giving of their time? They have daughters and sons, nieces and nephews, and younger colleagues, all of whom need to know how to succeed. They are also bosses who want you to be successful.

Why are there separate references to young women? While most of the discussion in this book is general business advice, some of it is specific to women, such as the chapter on appearance. Everyone knows that women are not well represented at senior levels in corporations and many service firms, and many people feel this is more than a pipeline issue. One partner in a major law firm confided that her firm hires 50/50 men/women out of law school, but after four years only 40 percent of the women were still there compared to 80 percent of the men. A number of women may have decided to leave because they did not like the firm, the practice of law, or for personal reasons, but all of them? Many believe that some women have a harder time understanding how to fit in to male-dominated organizations. This book will highlight areas where there may be differences between women and men. Men, do not put this book down because you assume it is a "woman's" book. You pass up this opportunity at your own risk: you probably have a lot to learn from these executives.

I thought that at some point the answers to the questions posed would become redundant. This didn't happen. Each woman had a unique perspective on at least one of the issues. Personally I learned a great deal from talking to them and only wish I had been able to tap their advice earlier in my career.

One note of caution: there is no one solution to your career challenges. Every person is different and not all of these suggestions will work for you. Take the advice that makes sense for you now and file away the other ideas for possible use in the future.

Two

Manage Your Own Career: No One Else Will

There is an unspoken understanding between the employer and the employee: neither one of you expects the relationship to last forever. Therefore, you cannot count on the company to manage your career. You need to think about what you want to get from your employer and what you need to do on your own.

- "When I walk out of a company, I want to have grown, enhanced my skill set, and be a more marketable person."
- "From the moment you start a job, prepare yourself for other internal and external opportunities."

A New Job Is a New Start

You just started a new job. Now what do you do? A new job is a wonderful opportunity to start fresh and become the professional you always wanted to be. The only opinions people have of you are the ones they formed in your job interviews, and they must have been positive or you would not have been offered the position. The first few weeks on the job are critical to creating your image in the new company or department, so use this time well.

- "You get a reputation very early and it sticks with you. You want to overdeliver and build from a strong position."
- "You want to get off on the right foot and be known as a hard worker. Then if you have a little setback, you have some cushion."

One thing to remember is that most companies have a lot of history, and it all happened before you got there. It is like opening a long novel in the middle: there are many characters with existing relationships, so do not assume you know everything. It is going to take you awhile to feel comfortable and understand the culture of the company and how it operates. Which teams in the company are aligned with each other? Who gets together after work with whom? Who used to date and which people can't stand to work together? Keep your antennae up and your opinions to yourself.

- "Do a lot of observing. How does the company really work? When do people come to work and when do they leave? You don't know who to emulate yet, so watch your boss and peers."
- "Make sure you understand the culture and the rules of engagement before you take the job."

What are some of the practical tips that will make your transition to the new job easier?

- "Get to know the key people in your department, starting with your job interview."
- "Learn about the business as quickly as you can. The best way to do this is by meeting with people in leadership positions inside and outside your department."
- "Your supervisor may have set up an orientation program, but if not, suggest ways that would help you learn to do your job."
- "If the former job holder is still with the company, talk to him or her to understand what is needed in the role."
- "Have lunch or coffee with coworkers in groups of two or three and ask them about their work."
- "Introduce yourself to people in the hall. Find reasons to meet people. Email people that you just want to say hello and drop by their offices so they can put a face with the name."
- "If you have an assistant, find out what support is provided for you. Ask your assistant how she or he would like to receive work from you."

Sometimes people have the best intentions but just get off on the wrong foot. What should you *not* do in a new company?

- "No one wants to hear someone say, 'We did this X way at my old company.' Try another approach to get the same idea across, such as 'I've had experience doing it this way before' or 'Have we thought about doing it this way?'"

✔ **Takeaways:** Create a strong first impression in a new job by working hard and making an effort to meet people. Be proactive in educating yourself about the company and your job. Do not compare things to your prior employer.

Hard Work Is Not Enough

The two most important things to understand about your career are that you must be very good at what you do and you must work incredibly hard. All the other advice that comes next is what you need to do after you have done these two critical things.

- "You must commit to great performance. A lot of people are not willing to make the sacrifices necessary. You need to invest the time, passion, and energy required to be very good at your job. Once you have great performance, then worry about getting noticed."
- "Don't expect to be promoted if you can't deliver the goods."
- "If you are not capable, you will not have a seat at the table. The entrance fee is hard work."
- "There is no substitution for hard work."

However, good work and long hours alone are not enough. One woman learned this very early in her career.

- "I got laid off my first job after 15 months. They had hired too many people and when business fell off, they fired two-thirds of my class. It was a rude awakening. I had gotten great performance reviews, but other people were better at promoting themselves, so they were better known."

- "In order to succeed you have to work hard, but it does not mean it will be appreciated, noticed, or rewarded."
- "You may add value to the institution, but you may not be valued by the institution."
- "It is a myth that if you work hard someone will reward you. It is like waiting to win the lottery."
- "You need to put in 130 percent. It's 80 percent hard work and 50 percent everything else."

How do you make sure that your work gets noticed by people? This can be especially difficult if you do not have much access to your boss in one-on-one situations.

- "You need to learn how to do self-promoting and networking that are consistent with your personality. Develop a fan club, people above and below you who will fight to work with you and will help promote you."
- "How well you do in a company is a popularity contest, real and perceived. You need to be your own marketing committee."
- "There are ways to quietly self-promote. Find a business reason to keep your boss up to speed on what you are doing. For example, one person here provides her boss with a database of all the calls she is making. Another one copies the boss on all the letters to prospects."
- "If your boss does not seem to take any notice, ask someone slightly more senior than yourself how to get her interest."

The key, of course, is to have people be aware of your work without making it look like you are working too hard on getting noticed.

- "You need to self-market, but you do not want to be viewed as the guy who pats himself on the back. So you do not want to say, 'Do you know that I did . . . ?' It is more effective to schedule a meeting with your boss and say, 'I am interested in getting your input on this project,' or 'These are some of the things my department has done.'"
- "True self-promotion is frowned upon, but you need to be sure people are looking."

- "You need to 'market' what you are doing, but not 'advertise.' Your peers will get annoyed if you say 'I did this,' but you can subtly let your boss know you are thinking strategically about the organization by saying something like 'I came across some information on X that I thought would interest you.'"

One of the best ways to get noticed is to have your firm's customers weigh in on your service.

- "If you have good relationships with customers, find a way for them to tell your boss how you are doing."

There may be cultural or geographic differences concerning what styles are effective in getting your work noticed at different companies.

- "On the East Coast, if you are not working nights and weekends, people think you have a bad work ethic. On the West Coast, everyone has the entrepreneurial spirit, so people are much more concerned about getting the job done than face time."
- "Be careful about self-promoting; it varies by work environment. One neutral way to be sure your work is seen is to give it to the person who requested it and ask him if it is what he wanted."

What are other things you need to take on before you can move up? You need to actively work to round out your skills. There is a certain amount of chance involved in your career, but you certainly want to be ready to take advantage of the opportunities available to you.

- "Remember the 80/20 rule. Do your main job in 80 percent of your time and spend 20 percent developing the attributes and skills you need to get ahead."
- "You need the right 'package': a strong work ethic and the ability to get things done; knowledge of how to present your ideas; good judgment; and luck—being in the right place at the right time."

✔ **Takeaways:** Being good at what you do and working hard are the most important parts of your job, but they are not enough to get you promoted. You need to be sure your work is noticed by others through subtle marketing efforts aimed at letting your boss and other people in the organization understand the value of your work.

Line versus Support

There are two broad classifications in any organization: departments that generate revenue (often called "line") and departments that "support" the line functions. For example, in a manufacturing organization, the line jobs are sales, research and development, and manufacturing, while the support jobs are finance, legal, human resources, and information technology.

The same skill set can be line or support, depending on the company. A "support" lawyer in a manufacturing company may be from a law firm where he was considered "line," and a "support" team member from finance may have been hired from an accounting firm where she was in a "line" assignment.

Every company needs all of its departments in order to deliver its products or services, and therefore each function is critical to the organization's success. However, the company culture determines the value placed on different departments. In many organizations, line people are considered more critical to the performance of the company than support people, who may be considered easier to replace. In these firms, line jobs are given more respect, paid more, and offered more opportunity for advancement.

Before you choose a career path you need to consider a number of factors, and a serious one is whether you are more comfortable in line or support, however these roles are defined in your company.

- "There is no right or wrong between line and support. It is just a question of what you like to do."
- "You need to be intellectually honest with yourself about what you want to do. What drives you: money, position, a feel-good environment?"

- "What skill sets are you good at and where do they fit in the organization?"
- "Line still has more cachet than support, but what do you think you would be better at? The most important thing is that you do well in whatever role you choose."
- "Certain personalities fit naturally into different jobs. In this firm the more outgoing people go into developing client relationships."

People move between line and support at different times in their careers, but movement is not always easy, so it needs to be carefully planned.

- "It is tough to get line responsibilities, so if you want to go that route, the sooner you jump in the better."
- "If you want line experience, you need to get it early. However, if you want to rise to the higher levels of a company, you need a good balance of line and support."
- "A line job is important. You need to be able to make money if you want a management role."
- "Sometimes a line person needs a rotation through a staff position to round out a skill. You might also get more exposure to senior management if the staff position is at headquarters."
- "I am primarily a line person, but I took a support job when I had kids because it allowed me to work part-time."
- "If you have ambitions for a senior management job, you need to figure out how to get good experience in both strategic and tactical issues."

Individuals seem to naturally gravitate toward the areas they like best. The sooner you consider the differences between line and support in your company and where you will be most successful, the sooner you can get on the right path for you.

- "Pay attention to where you feel the most satisfied professionally, where you feel intellectually challenged, where you feel a personality fit."

- "Eighty percent of a line job is detail and implementation, and some people find that too slow. Personally, I prefer a line job since I never felt I was building anything in a support job."
- "I started out in support, but it was not what I wanted to do. I moved to a line job because I wanted to be responsible for all the decisions and to see a project through to the end."
- "On the line you are responsible for generating revenue or bringing in business. The hours are often less controllable, and it can be stressful."

Many people felt that line is a better place to be than staff, especially for women.

- "Women do better where there is a scorecard. When you have the numbers, all the 'soft stuff' is less important."
- "Staff jobs are mostly filled by women at our firm, and they do not pay as well."

However, line jobs have personal and professional risks as well, so you cannot assume that because you are making money for your firm you will always have a job.

- "The only way to eliminate qualitative judgment about your performance is to know something very well. The problem is that if you are an expert in a subject, you may get bored intellectually. Also, if you have a one-track expertise and do not get to run the business, you will have to leave if you want to get ahead or are in an up-or-out culture."

While it may sound as if there is a bias toward line jobs, there were many people who had opted for support positions and thoroughly enjoyed their roles. This was especially true for individuals who had moved from line positions in professional service firms to a client where they were in a support department.

- "When I was in a line position I felt like all I did was fight fires. Now that I am in a support job I have time to think more strategically. Personally, I think I have a greater impact on the bottom line than I did in my old job."

- "I was in a professional services firm where I generated revenue, but I felt that all I did was move from transaction to transaction and it started to feel very repetitive. I went to a company where my position is considered support, but I am much more involved in the business. I bring a way of looking at problems they never considered before, and I am helping the company grow and expand."

One person felt very strongly that many women opt into support jobs because they are not willing to make the investments in their careers necessary to move into top line positions.

- "Once women have survived four to five years they start asking themselves what is the return going to be on the incremental investment they need to make to meet the challenges that lie ahead of them. It is at this point that organizations get more stratified and there is more pay-for-performance. You need to be better at attributes that often are considered 'male,' such as being more assertive. Women often don't score well in that area and rather than working on what they need to know, just move out of the roles where new skills are needed."

She went on to say that many women assume the trade-off of pay will result in a better lifestyle, and since they assume they will get married and have kids, this is a good trade. However, what if everything does not work out as planned?

- "Women need to be more broad-minded in their thinking. What if there is no spouse, or your spouse dies or leaves you? Can you take care of yourself or elderly parents or children?"

✔ **Takeaways:** Whether you decide to choose a line or a support job, it should fit your personality and be a position in which you can be successful. You can always move from line to support, but if you want line experience, you need to get it early in your career. Many people feel line jobs are better than support jobs since they have objective scorecards. However, a significant group feels that support jobs offer more opportunity to think away from the crisis mentality often seen in line positions.

Map Your Own Career Path

You should think of your job as a stepping-stone in your career. You want more than just a paycheck for the hours you spend at work. One person expressed this very well.

- "My career is an important part of who I am."

No two people are exactly the same, and every person's career will be a little different. There are no right or wrong answers.

- "Your job is to find your voice in a complicated environment. We are not all going to get there the same way. The key is to be effective."
- "Choose a style and approach that you can stay with for the long run."

The days of trusting your boss or company to manage this part of your life are long gone, if they ever existed at all. Chances are you will change companies at least several times, and even if you stay with one company your entire career, you will move through different departments. While you may consult people within your own company for internal opportunities, remember that everyone has different objectives. They may be telling you what would be good for their own career or what they think you need to hear so they can fill an open slot.

- "Most companies are passive about managing their employees' careers."
- "Anyone who does not 'own' her career will not be successful in the long run."
- "No one cares more about your career than you do. There is not a mother or father figure to take care of you."
- "There is no secret file in the human resources department with your name and your next three jobs."
- "Others only think about what is in the best interests of the company."
- "To the company it is all business. Is there a common ground between what the person wants and the company needs?"

That is not to say that your current boss does not impact your career and may not have some good input.

- "Most promotions are based on performance and potential. You need to show a glimmer of potential to be considered for promotion. However, do not send signals that you are not interested in your current job."
- "Have a meeting with your boss and tell her what you are doing, where you want to go, and how you plan to get there. Keep notes from the meeting and refer to them regularly to be sure you are on track."
- "Talk to your boss about future plans, but don't be so interested in your career path that he thinks you are not focused on the job you are doing now."

Some companies have very clear career paths, especially in the early years.

- "At our firm there is a clear understanding of what the promotion milestones are, what skills are needed when, and how you develop them."
- "If you work at a company with a 'high potential' list, find out if you are on it and if not, why not. Can you be

considered for special training programs the company may
have for people they expect to move up?"

Professional service firms are often the most challenging places to
manage a career. The key problems are how to get staffed on the
"right" deals and how to juggle the demands of the different projects
on which you are staffed.

- "You may or may not know what the best experience is.
  This is where you can draw on the expertise of your mentors for advice."
- "In professional service firms you have competing demands.
  How you say you are overworked is important. Some partners you can say no to, and others you can't. Go to a mentor first with the issue and ask advice on how to solve the
  problem."
- "You need to pick the right projects and learn the tips and
  tricks of saying no. A colleague or mentor may be helpful
  in figuring this out."
- "You better have a good excuse if you can't get the work
  done. Your wedding is sacred, but the delivery of a chair
  is not."

Building client relationships is a skill that all people in professional
service firms need to develop and is an important part of managing your career. Even if you work in a corporation you have clients:
they are the people you support or senior management.

- "You need to develop into a trusted adviser and counselor.
  The biggest problem young people have is focusing on
  their relationship with the junior client, with whom they
  may feel more comfortable, rather than the most senior
  person, such as the CEO, who might be more intimidating."
- "Remember that there needs to be a 'fit' between you and
  your client. I was staffed on a team with a CEO who just
  did not like me. I asked off the team, but my team leader
  was very comfortable with my work and insisted I stay.
  When we had a blowup with the client it suddenly became

my fault. If the chemistry is not right, get reassigned as soon as you can."

How far ahead should you plan your career? Most people do not look further than five years.

- "You need a sense of where you want to be in the next three to five years. Ask yourself if you are on the right path and what else you need to do."
- "I plan on changing jobs every three years. Many of my jobs were in the same company, but I needed to find ways to stay fresh."
- "Think of your career objectives as near term, medium term, and long term. Jobs and companies change frequently so you can't plan exactly, but what general direction are you headed in? What do you really aspire to?"

Not everyone looks very far out, and some do no advance planning.

- "Don't plan ahead, but when you see an opportunity, seize it. Windows only open for a short period."
- "I know you are supposed to look ahead five years, but in reality I have been a just-in-time planner."
- "The only time to plan your career is when it is not working."

You may not plan very far ahead because you are ambivalent about some areas of your job, but do not share these concerns at work or people will not want to invest their time and energy to help you.

- "I tend not to think more than one to two years out. There is such a high personal cost to what I do that I will have to consider every few years if I am still having a great time and still learning."

What issues should you consider in planning your career? There is a long list.

- "I manage a large group of associates and I am amazed at their short-term mentality. This may be their first job, but

it won't be their last. They need to ask themselves the basic
career questions. What do you want out of this job? How
do you maximize your opportunity in this position? Do you
want to stay a long time, or is this a stepping-stone? You
can't rely on anyone else to do this thinking for you."

■ "People should realize there is no defined career ladder.
Think of the skills you want, not the title."

■ "When you are young, you have a lot of alternatives and
can change departments. There is a risk, though, of becoming a jack-of-all-trades and a master of none, and then no
one will think you are qualified to run anything."

■ "You need to think about where your family plans fit into
your career planning."

What skills do you need to develop? How do you get that training?
That will depend on the company and what is available to you.

■ "Think about what skills you need to compete for your
next assignment. Leverage what you know, but be humble
enough to know what you don't know."

■ "Nail your existing job in the first six months and after
that start thinking about your next promotion. What do
you need to learn, and how can you subtly acquire new
skills?"

■ "I asked myself, 'What do I need to get out of my comfort
zone?' For example, I was not good at public speaking, so
I went looking for speaking opportunities."

■ "I came in through the finance department, and every
time I applied for a job in another part of the company, I
was told I was not qualified. Rather than get my master's
in finance, I got it in communications, which opened up
many other areas of opportunities."

■ "The only way you will ever be successful is to be a lifelong learner. If there is no course, teach yourself."

Don't be afraid to be aggressive and let people know you want to
get ahead. Sitting quietly at your desk may not get you the promotion you deserve.

- "One of the worst mistakes I made was when my boss asked me what I wanted to do next, and I said I liked what I was doing and wanted to stay. What I did not know was that he was about to add another layer of management, so I ended up reporting to a new person who was brought in between me and my old boss. That job could have been mine if I had just let him know I was interested."
- "I looked at the training programs people two levels above me were getting. I asked my boss if I could go and I made a good case was to why it made sense. I did not get in the first group, but I got in the second group."

People have different ways of doing their career planning, and it rarely is a formal process.

- "You should always be focused on your next steps."
- "Have a plan for the next two to three years. Be disciplined and set concrete goals. Just don't be so focused on executing the plan that you miss other opportunities that come up."
- "This is where the old boys' network has helped men. Women need to develop informal channels. This is a place you need to let your interests be known."
- "Every New Year's Eve Day my sisters and I get together, sit around in pajamas, and plan the next year. I ask myself, 'What do I want my life to look like and feel like?' I write it all down. It encompasses things ranging from what I want my job to be like to making great tomato sauce."

It is great to have a single-minded focus on your career, but what if you do not know what you want to do? Take time to look at job postings on your own company's and other Web sites, reading the job descriptions carefully. Consider what you like and do not like about your current position and what types of jobs use more of the things you enjoy doing. Even eliminating possibilities is career planning.

- "Think broadly about how your skills can be used. If you like dealing with people, don't go straight to human resources, consider sales or customer service, which may offer more career mobility and pay better."

Several women mentioned that there can be differences in the way men and women think about a career, and those differences sometimes work to a woman's disadvantage.

- "Men never think about dropping out, but many women are constantly thinking of leaving. This lack of commitment affects how much energy they are willing to put into career planning."
- "I was divorced with young kids early in my career, and people always tell me it must have been hard. In fact, I think it made it easier since I never had a choice about working. If I didn't work, the mortgage wouldn't be paid."

Sometimes the best way to get ahead is to take risks and stretch yourself.

- "You need to be willing to go places and do things others are not willing to do."
- "Often the jobs I was talked into doing were the best jobs I ever had."
- "Sometimes I have taken a job I did not want to round out a skill set I needed to get ahead."
- "A few times I went where I was told and took jobs I would rather not have taken. It was scary sometimes and I would go home and complain, but I got great experience."
- "Take risks. Do things off the beaten path."
- "Whoever has the best experiences wins."

Careers rarely work out as planned, but everyone seems to adjust to the changed circumstances. You just need to keep moving forward.

- "There were many points in my career when I was not able to do what I wanted to do. I did not get into my first choice business school. The transfer overseas did not happen. Even if things do not work out as expected, in the long run it is your determination that matters in your success."

■ "Sometimes you just have to suck it up when things do not turn out the way you want."

✔ **Takeaways:** Look forward three to five years in your career. Consider where you want to go and what training you need to get there. Make your interests known to your boss. Be willing to take risks to round out your experience. If you do not know what you want to do, research other jobs and consider what you enjoy and what motivates you to do well.

Listen Carefully to Criticism

In order to be better at what you do, you need to get feedback and get it often. This is one place I intentionally asked a leading question: "Women have a reputation for not taking criticism well. Do you think this is true?" The overwhelming answer was amusing: no one likes criticism, and no one takes it well. Therefore, if you can figure out how to use this important information that people are trying to give you, then you will be viewed as much more professional than your peers.

■ "I have two high performers reporting to me. One gets very defensive when I give him criticism, and it's a real turnoff. The other takes it very well, and I feel it is refreshing that she is willing to tackle the issue rather than just shutting down."

■ "When you make it easy for people to give you criticism, you will become a joint product and they will feel more invested."

■ "Successful individuals need to learn how to take criticism well. It is good to show you take it seriously."

■ "Some people want everyone to like them, and they take criticism much too seriously. You'll never learn if you don't get feedback. This is not your social life. This is your job."

- "People who don't like criticism try to narrow their field of work to an area where they know they can be successful. This is a mistake."

Formal reviews are an excellent time to get detailed feedback about your performance, so approach the review with an open mind.

- "This is an opportunity, so embrace it. Don't dwell on what you have done wrong but on how to do better in the future. Walk away knowing what you need to change."
- "You should be thankful your boss is articulating feedback you can act on."
- "You are lucky to be getting criticism, since most people do not take the time. Make sure you understand the point. Make it comfortable for the person giving you the advice."
- "When someone criticizes you, it is either reality or their perception, but in either case you need to fix it."

What mistakes have people seen others make in performance reviews? One thing that was mentioned was never to highlight your own faults to people. The other is to be careful how you respond. Don't give a written response that will end up in your file. Down the road someone could read it out of context, and you might look like a complainer.

- "I have a brilliant woman working for me and when she turned in her self-evaluation that asked for three positives and three negatives, even her positives were negative. She has no confidence and said she just wanted to get it all off her chest. Everyone is a work in progress, but you do not need to tell people all your flaws. If you need to find negatives, think of wording them as things you still need to learn rather than what you do not know."
- "If the criticism is wrong, you should respond to it, but never in writing. Wait until the next day when you can think about it clearly and logically tell your boss why you disagree."

You can easily get feedback from your boss outside of formal reviews, and it can often be more effective since there is no pressure associated with the conversation.

- "Go in when things are going well and ask, 'What would you like me to do more of and what would you like me to do less of?'"
- "Ask your boss, 'How am I doing?'"
- "Asking how you are doing lets you improve your performance, and if you are off track you can get back on quickly."

There are times when you make a major mistake and you get—and deserve—strong criticism. How should you react?

- "Sometimes you screw up and someone is very angry. This is the time for a mea culpa. Tell the person he is absolutely right and you won't do it again."
- "You have to be accountable for your mistakes. Sometimes the best strategy is a well-oiled reverse. Saying you are sorry works well in diffusing the anger."
- "You can't be successful without making some major mistakes. Some people are not used to coming back after a visible failure, but remember that this is what happens in sports every day."

Some of the best feedback can come informally from people other than your boss, so reach out to other people as well.

- "Get feedback from your peers or people who are more junior than you. They often see things you did not."
- "Ask for criticism after meetings. Ask other attendees what you did right and wrong. It makes people comfortable about giving you criticism."
- "After a presentation, circle back with people and ask them what else they would like to have heard."

You may be in a situation where you are working with someone who does not take any suggestions or criticism. If that person is senior to you, you may need to find ways to make that person adopt your ideas as her own.

- "I had a boss who could not take head-on challenges, so I would word things as questions: 'Do you think we should consider this?' or 'Should we look at that?' We all joked about it when she wasn't there, but we got our points across."

Some people thought women reacted to criticism differently than men. Since these people bring their own prejudices into the room when they are giving a review, if you are a woman you may need to make even more of an effort to be professional when receiving criticism.

- "Women fear failure more than they desire success. They take criticism very personally, and it is all tied up in their sense of self-worth."
- "Women are worse than men at taking criticism and worse on forgiving. Some women do not like to work with people who criticize them."
- "Women take criticism personally. Men get defensive."
- "Women tend to bristle at off-the-cuff comments. They are more responsive to thoughtful criticism."
- "Women need their advice more gently. They need to know the reviewer cares."
- "When a review does not go well, a woman blames herself and a man blames the circumstances."

✓ **Takeaways:** Criticism can be extremely useful to help you improve your performance. Seek out feedback and be receptive to comments from others.

Graduate School

If you are in an industry where you need a graduate degree to move up, the question is always when to get your degree. There are a variety of opinions, and the answer depends on the type of degree you need. Business schools prefer some work experience, but law and other graduate schools will accept people right after college.

- "You should never get a business degree right out of college. You need to work for a while."
- "I got my master's in engineering directly after college, and I am glad I did. That way I was not trying to do everything simultaneously."
- "Two to five years after college is a good time to get a business degree."
- "Get your second degree in your 20s. As you get older, the opportunity cost gets higher and you start having more family demands."
- "In general, people go back too early. You can assimilate more in graduate school after you have some work experience to draw on."

A number of people mentioned that the best of all options is to keep working while you get your degree, especially if you can get your company to pay some of the tuition. Many people cannot afford to be without a salary for the time it takes to complete a degree. However, you also need to consider whether you can juggle night and weekend courses and continue to do well in your job.

- "If you can manage it, go at night."
- "If you can get the company to pay for your degree, that is the best solution. Then they feel they have a big investment in you."
- "I got my degree at night before I had kids. I just could not afford to stop working."

Do you really need another degree? It depends on what you want to do since degree requirements are industry and job specific. In some companies you need to have an advanced degree to be taken seriously for management positions.

- "On paper it was not clear I needed an MBA, but it afforded me a level of flexibility in my career that I would not have had without it."

- "Someone I know who is looking for a general management position told me that even after all his great experience, what impresses people most is where he went to law school. You would think at some point degrees would not matter, but they do."

Other people use school as a way to leave a job and look for something new.

- "Sometimes you have stopped learning in your job, and graduate school is a great opportunity to take a break."

✔ **Takeaways:** Consider working several years before going to graduate school. If you can go at night, your employer may pay part of the tuition. An advanced degree will often provide you with opportunities that would otherwise not be available.

When to Leave

It is always difficult to leave a job, especially if you like your co-workers. However, you may feel that you have been in one place too long or are not getting the opportunities you deserve. How do you decide to leave? There are lots of subtle signs that you are in the wrong place.

- "You need to be happy in your job, respect the people you work with, and be intellectually challenged. When you are missing one or more of these elements, it is time to find something else."
- "It's time to leave when I'm no longer getting respect, and people take what I am doing for granted."
- "Go with your gut if you feel you are not at the right organization. Your gut processes lots of cues you cannot articulate."
- "You need to work for someone who values your skill set. Chances are, if your skills are very different from those of your boss, then he will not value you and not promote you."

- "We all know when things are not working out. If someone starts acquiring the aura of a loser, then it's too late. He should have left earlier."
- "Sometimes the organizational needs just do not fit with your plans."

If you want to move internally, how long do you need to stay in one department?

- "In this company, we value loyalty. If someone has been in a job 12 months or more, I consider her 'fair game' for an internal move. If she wants to go after less than a year, she looks like an opportunist and I know she is not a player."

One issue to consider is whether your current company's perception of you has changed as you have gained new skills, or whether the organization still sees you in your original role.

- "If you have been in one organization for a long time, it is often better to leave. Usually they do not see you as the person you have grown into."

One person raised an issue about perceptions that others did not agree with, but it is worth noting in case your company or boss fits this category.

- "It is often better to leave a company where you have had children. They have seen you at your most vulnerable and will always remember you as pregnant."

People always assume there are risks in leaving a job, but there are also risks involved in staying in one place for a long time.

- "If you stay at one company too long, especially a large company, people will think you are set in your ways and will not adapt to a new environment well."
- "I was a consultant and since I wanted to end up in a line job at a company, I had to ask myself whether was it worth the extra years to get to be a partner. I decided no,

since those extra years of consulting would not help me in
my line experience, and I left."
- "I made the mistake of staying in one job too long and I
got stale. I got trapped into thinking that my skills were
limited to that industry. I finally got more proactive and
got out."

If you are considering leaving your current position or have been
let go, there is always the question of what type of company you
should look for next and what type of job.

- "You want the 'academy-like' names, big successful companies, on your résumé early. You can usually go from a
big company to a small company, but it is hard to go from
a small company to a larger one, since people will not believe that you have had the right training."
- "Don't be afraid to say that you don't like it and find something that works for you. I was an associate at a law firm,
had no control over my time, and it was a very lonely job.
I was much happier when I became an in-house lawyer."

When you are unhappy, other opportunities always look better, but
consider all the downsides of another job or company before you
move. Try to figure out why you are not happy in your current job
and see if you can change the situation.

- "I was offered a high-level staff job at a very prestigious
company that would report to a highly regarded CEO. I
was about to take it when I thought about whether I would
really fit in. The CEO held a lot of the meetings with his
senior staff on weekends, often over a golf game at a remote location, when I was used to spending weekends with
my husband and children. My next move at the company
would have to be in a line job and I was not sure I wanted
that. Finally, even if I took a line job, all their plants were
in rural locations, and I did not think my husband could
get a job there. I realized it was a great opportunity for
someone, just not for me."
- "Leave to go to something, not to escape something."

Sometimes people just get fed up or are exhausted and want to get out. This may not be the right decision if it is based on a short-term situation. Take a vacation first to see if you just need some time off.

- "I tell junior people, 'Don't stay or leave if you have a bad day. If over the long term it does not feel good, then you should leave.'"
- "I came home one day and told my daughter I wanted to quit. She said to me, 'Mommy, don't quit after one bad day. If you have a lot of bad days, then maybe you should quit.'"
- "People are like race cars. You can't run on red all the time and expect that extra power will be there when you need it. People can burn out, so pace yourself."
- "I've seen very successful people leave because they feel like failures. Sometimes there are tough projects that grind you down. You need a long-term perspective. This is when you go talk to other people."

Often people try to improve a difficult situation. While this is admirable, it is not always possible. Sometimes you just need to leave.

- "When you join a company, you sign up for their culture. If you do not like it, you need to realize you are not going to change the culture."
- "Sometimes a woman says, 'I am going to make this work' when she has a difficult boss or finds herself in a no-win situation, whereas a man would say, 'This is not worth my time.'"
- "Often it is just better to jump ship and find a better opportunity or a more positive work environment."
- "Don't be afraid of failing. Sometimes you need to move to grow."

The choice to leave is not always your own, and it may or may not be related to your performance.

- "Here, we tell people when to leave. It is all a matter of supply and demand. If the firm is busy and you are not, there is a reason. You need to address this problem or leave. If people fight to get you, you are successful."

- "Many times the company is downsizing and it has nothing to do with your capabilities."

So you have been fired, now what do you do?

- "As hard as it is, get the emotion out of it as early as you can. Act professionally. Go out with class. They might come to regret they let you go, especially if it was a cutback."
- "Make sure there is a smooth transition of duties to the new person. It will enhance your reputation if you handle yourself well. Your new employer will respect you as well if you can talk about what you did as you left."
- "Try to negotiate your reference before you leave. In today's world, many companies will officially just confirm the time of your employment and your salary. It is unlikely you can get more in writing, but often your boss will talk to prospective employers if you are on good terms when you leave."

One thing that may be obvious, but is worth repeating, is to leave your current company or department on good terms.

- "Don't burn any bridges. People move around these days, and you never know when you will end up working with these people again."
- "Leave the company on excellent terms. Never say anything negative in an exit interview. Walk around and shake hands with people."
- "There is an old saying that you can lose friends, but enemies stay with you forever."

Even if you are happy in your current assignment and are not actively looking, should you consider listening to opportunities when they present themselves? Most people think it is a good idea to know your market value, but you may not want to let people at the company know you talk to headhunters since they might misinterpret your interest.

- "Talk to headhunters. Never be rude to them. Listen. Understand what is happening in the market in your field, and give them names of others if you are not interested."
- "Always evaluate options and opportunities. Don't keep your head in the sand."
- "Always have a current résumé and people willing to act as references."
- "Being opportunistic is valuable."
- "I have never actively looked for a job, but I have been recruited away. I would not do a lateral move, but I would leave for significantly greater compensation, a much bigger title, or an opportunity to showcase my expertise."

✔ Takeaways: Do not stay in one job too long or you will get stale. Don't quit if you've had a bad week, but leave if you are in the wrong place. Talk to headhunters periodically and always have a current résumé. Keep your eyes open for internal and external opportunities.

■ Career-Enhancing Moves

1. Manage your career. Look at where you want to go over the next three years and get the experience and training you need to get there.
2. Educate yourself on the company, its business, and clients when you start a new job.
3. Get line experience early in your career.
4. Actively seek out feedback on your performance and listen to criticism in a professional, nonemotional way.
5. Leave a company when you are not moving up or are taken for granted.
6. Market yourself in subtle ways so that people understand your value to the organization.

■ Career–Limiting Moves

1. Do not assume someone else will be managing your career for you.
2. Do not think you can change a company's culture. If you do not fit in, it's time to leave.
3. Do not build a career solely in support jobs if you want to rise to a senior management position.

Three

The Key to Effective Communications: Get to the Point

One complaint I heard repeatedly from the women I interviewed was that many people do not have good communications skills. Whether you are sending an email, talking on the phone, participating in a meeting, or giving a formal presentation, you need to get the issues across effectively. If you want to be sure your ideas are understood and you get credit for them, you must express yourself well. Very few people work alone in business, so you will spend your career explaining your work to others and need to be able to communicate clearly and concisely.

Focus Your Communications

Some people feel that women can be less focused and take longer to get to the point than men. Others feel this is more a function of personality than of gender.

- "On average, women tend to be more verbose than men."
- "Women are more likely to process out loud, rather than process in their heads and then speak."
- "Women are interested in telling you all the steps. Men are more interested in the punch line."
- "Women in my business are tough as nails. They key in on the right issues."

How you communicate overall has a major impact on what people think of you. Focus your communications and get to the issues at hand. Just because you have analytical or technical skills, you cannot assume this will be enough.

- "We hire all these people who are very analytical but lack verbal skills. The problem is that you need to be able to speak well and communicate to move ahead."
- "A woman I know told us everything she thought about while working on the issue. Since she could never focus, I could not recommend her for promotion."
- "Some people just throw out lots of ideas to get credit for thinking of them. I can see through that."

There are many good ways to express issues in written and oral form, so let's explore some of them.

Written Communication Must Be Concise

Whether you are using email or a memo, most people want the conclusion or most important information first, so they know if they need to take the time to read more. In any event, the writing should be concise.

- "Certain people, such as lawyers or accountants, are linear thinkers and want to take you from point A to point B, et cetera, so that you understand all their logic. The problem is I don't want all that detail. Start with your conclusions and then provide a summary of how you got there. If I want complete details, I'll ask."
- "The memo or presentation should be logical and well ordered, starting with the summary, then the background."
- "I keep my memos to one page and put any needed backup in an appendix."
- "Use short bullets. Long prose is less effective."
- "Less is more."

How and where people are reading the information will impact how long the communication should be. Often people are checking email on the run between meetings and simply do not have much time.

- "Everyone here uses handhelds to pick up email when traveling. If the email is too long, I just am not going to read it."

People have a tendency to write something and just send it out, but it is critical to spend the extra time on your written work to make sure it is professional.

- "It is particularly important in a written document to edit your work."
- "Look at your written work and judge its clarity, content, and tone. Be sure you have covered the basics such as good grammar, punctuation, and spelling."
- "Writing is one of your first chances to demonstrate your judgment skills. You might make a substantive mistake, but at least think about what you have written before you send it out."

Look at the communication from the perspective of the reader to be sure it is clear and there is no ambiguity about what response you would like from the recipient.

- "Too often people wonder why someone did not get back to them, but if they only reread the memo or email they would see it was not clear that a reply was expected."
- "People don't always 'frame up' the subject for someone. Are you just giving him information or are you asking for an opinion? Make it clear up front."

Your analysis should respond to the issues at hand. If a recommendation is expected, make sure you have one that is thoughtful and can be implemented.

- "A client said it very clearly: 'When a guy has his head up a buffalo's ass, don't tell him how he got there. Tell him how to get it out.'"
- "Young people tend to offer factual information rather than an action plan. Don't ask me what to do. Give me a solution to the problem."
- "Focus on the conclusions and recommendations first and any inherent risks in the recommendations."
- "I see a lot of memos telling me which numbers went up

and which went down, but I can see that for myself. What I want to know is why."

- "I had a client who used to say, 'Tell me something I don't already know.'"

Good business writing skills can be critical to your career, and over and over people said that younger people underestimate how important writing skills can be. If you want to move up, you need to learn to write well. It just takes some extra time.

- "Write your emails and memos as if you had the job you want to have. If you send disciplined, focused, buttoned-up emails, it will signal that you are a serious professional, there to contribute."
- "Unless you are a successful writer, you will not advance."
- "At my company we rate people on their 'strategic use of communications.'"
- "Writing a good memo is a real art form. I am shocked at how many educated people do not write well."
- "We had a man here who was very smart but just could not write well. He was constantly making grammatical mistakes. One of the senior managers said we should get rid of him since it was obvious he was not smart and would never be a candidate for any higher-level positions."

A common caution was about the tone of emails and memos. Many people are surprised at how their words can be misinterpreted.

- "Read your emails back with a different tone of voice to see if they can be misinterpreted. I sent someone an email asking for a list 'if he didn't mind,' and while I thought I was just being polite, he thought I was being sarcastic."
- "What I perceived to be direct, some people here viewed as nasty. I had to change my style."
- "Phrases such as 'Didn't we already discuss this?' in an email can be seen as confrontational."
- "Don't use all capital letters. People will think that you are yelling."

Even the choice of who gets copied on an email or a memo can send a strong signal, so be sure you know the unwritten company rules.

- "Whether you use email or memos is culturally idiosyncratic. Here we use email internally but memos for clients. The one exception is when we have a significant event. That warrants a real memo."
- "I worked at an organization that wanted to be inclusive, so people copied the world on emails. In other organizations, people do not want to be inundated. Follow the convention of your company."
- "In some companies, knowledge is power, and very few people get copied."

Writing styles also vary by company, so when you join a company, read some other emails before you start sending your own.

- "Look for examples in your company of how people address each other in written form. Do they use Sue, Susan, or Ms. Smith?"
- "Here we write an email just as if it is a letter."
- "Do people say 'I' or 'we'? Are there key words used frequently such as 'franchise'"?

There was a lot of caution about the format and content of email. The feeling is that while email has replaced the written memo for most business communication, people pay much less attention to the quality and professionalism of their emails than a letter or memo. This is usually a big mistake.

- "Ask yourself, 'Would the person I most admire at the company send out this email?'"
- "Treat an email like a letter. Use complete sentences, fix grammatical errors, and avoid text-messaging shorthand."
- "Don't underestimate the font choice for memos and emails. Some fonts are just not professional. Never use a colored background, and always have a signature block

with your name, title, address, phone number, and email address on the bottom."
- "Watch the cute factor in email. What does !!!! mean in a business email?"

The timing of sending an email can be important if you want it to be read carefully. Most senior professionals work on the weekend, and this is a great time to get mindshare.

- "Senior people tend to catch up over the weekend, so if an email arrives by Sunday midafternoon, it is likely to be read in a relaxed atmosphere and a response sent the same day."

Never forget that email has unintended legal and career risks. It is important to consider this fact before you hit the send button.

- "People misuse and abuse email in a profound way. They are not thoughtful about what they write and forget that email survives forever."
- "You need to be very careful what you say, and I've seen a lot of people get in trouble with email. People get way too casual and forget it is company property."
- "Everyone knows a story about someone hitting the 'reply to all' button when they just meant to make a wisecrack to a friend."
- "Once colleagues leave the firm they become outsiders. Do not forward any email to former coworkers that was not intended for public viewing."
- "When I am writing an email on a sensitive subject, I always ask myself what it would look like if it were re-printed in the newspaper."

Many people admitted to writing emails they regretted. You need to develop a system to control yourself so that you do not send something you want to recall later.

- "I have seen a lot of 'flame mails' that are just awful. I have adopted a 24-hour rule if I am angry. I type it up but put it in my draft file, and many times when I reread it the next day, I either rewrite it or delete it."

- "I once wrote an angry email to a client and when I hit the send button the computer froze. I think God was looking out for me."
- "Don't send emails when you are overtired or jet-lagged. They will contain mistakes."

✔ **Takeaways:** Memos and emails should be concise, with the most important information and any recommendations up front. Emails are professional communications, and you should pay close attention to grammar, spelling, and tone. Never send an email when tired or angry, since it may be less professional than it should be.

Email Should Not Replace All Human Contact

Email is a great tool, but it is not a substitute for human interaction. For many people, email has almost replaced picking up the phone or dropping by someone's office. However, there are many advantages to a phone call, even if you have to leave a voice mail.

- "Voice mail is so much better than email for a nuanced message. You can use pauses and the tone of your voice to convey exactly what you want to say."
- "By using a phone call you can soften a hard message. Email is very efficient, but it can come across as rude."
- "It is much more meaningful to thank someone on the phone or leave a congratulatory voice mail."
- "A phone call is a good way to develop a relationship with a boss, client, or peer, since it is much more personal than email."

For some people, a conversation in person is the best way to communicate. While you may think email is easy, a quick conversation can often get the job done faster. People cannot ignore you, and they are forced to respond.

- "Verbal communication is still the best. Plan it out before you go in. Take five minutes to say it quickly and get up and leave when you are finished. That way people won't roll their eyes when they see you coming."
- "Anything subtle needs to be handled with a live conversation."
- "There are times you need to talk to someone, and the back-and-forth of email will just not do. Schedule a time to talk."

Many people do not know how to use the phone well. Here are some specific suggestions on how to have an effective phone presence.

- "I always have a tight script with three bullet points ready before I get on the phone."
- "Answer your phone with your full name. Never answer on a speaker phone. It is not flattering, and your caller may find it pompous."
- "When leaving a voice mail, I stand up to give my voice more authority."

Voice mail is useful, but only if you make it simple for the person picking up the message. Remember, the recipient may be at an airport or between meetings.

- "I have told my team that when they leave me a voice mail to net it out right up front, so I can just listen to the first few words and know if I can save it for later or need to listen further."
- "Voice mail is like a short presentation: who is calling, what I want, and what I want you to do. You can be friendly and succinct at the same time."
- "Provide your phone number and name slowly both at the beginning and end of the call. If I do not know you, please spell your name. Do not assume I understood you."

Voice mail, like email, has legal consequences, and you need to remember this before you leave the message.

- "Whatever you say, you had better be sure you do not mind if it is recorded and passed on. I had a client use a voice mail against me early in my career, and I have never forgotten it."

✔ **Takeaways:** Use the phone or a personal meeting when you have a difficult message to deliver to avoid being misunderstood. Phone calls are an excellent way to offer congratulations, since you can express enthusiasm. When using voice mail, be succinct and before you dial have bullet points ready for the message you want to communicate.

Ubiquitous Technology Can Have Unintended Consequences

You can inadvertently leave a bad impression with your communications outside of the workplace.

- "Pick a nondescript personal email account name, since you might be sending emails from home. One woman in our office had such an offensive personal email address that some people in our office felt she should be fired. She was not let go, but it forever changed people's impressions of her."
- "Everyone knows your office voice mail message should be professional, but your cell phone and home messages should also be short and simple. I am amazed that some people have either weird or cute messages. It impacts how I think about someone."
- "If you have a blog, be careful what you post. Colleagues from work as well as recruiters may look at those."
- "Watch out what you have as your 'away' message on instant messaging. The language you used in college may not be acceptable in the business world."

✔ **Takeaways:** You will be communicating from home with business colleagues, so be sure your messages and home email address reflect the level of professionalism you maintain in the office.

Use Meetings to Get Noticed

A business meeting can take many forms. Whether you are a participant or presenter, you need to think in advance about the role you want to play. The most critical thing about a meeting is to be prepared and know the material being discussed.

- "Be prepared. Do your homework. This gives you a leg up on other people."
- "Always be prepared to speak, even if you are not expecting to."

If you just sit there while other people at your level are talking, you will not make a positive impression, so speak up early and be sure you are noticed.

- "Most business performance is oral, so if you do not talk, people will think you have no value."
- "Speak early so that your presence is known. Say something substantive, not just reinforcing what someone else said. That way, you will be included in the rest of the meeting and be taken seriously."
- "Get on the board. Say something in the first half hour, or you will be too terrified to speak later. Not to speak is terrible behavior."
- "You need to say a few things crisply. This makes you sound powerful."
- "Open your mouth at least once. At a minimum, introduce yourself to people as they come in so that they recognize your presence."

However, don't talk too much, and think about when to speak and for how long. While this sounds contradictory, there is a fine balance between speaking too little and too much, and it will differ for each meeting.

- "Gauge the time you are talking. You want to say enough meaningful things so that people look forward to your comments, but not so much that you hog air time."
- "I had a colleague who always spoke too much in meetings, but she recognized this and asked for help. We agreed on a subtle hand signal I would give her when she started to run on."
- "People kill themselves with one gratuitous comment that undoes all the positive things they have said."
- "When 10 people are sitting around, there is a tendency to chime in, but don't talk unless you have something important to say."
- "Don't be the first one to start talking. Be cognizant of the pecking order."
- "Find out if your peer group will be talking in the meeting. If they are not talking, then do not participate unless a senior person asks you to speak."

It is not always easy for someone to talk in meetings. It may be hard to jump in, or it may not be something you are comfortable doing. You need to get over the fear of speaking in meetings if you want to be taken seriously.

- "Women are taught to be polite and not interrupt. They do not like to cut people off, so they wait for an opening and it may never come."
- "It is still difficult for me to talk in large meetings. I work better one-on-one, but I know I must talk at the larger meetings."
- "In some company cultures you need to step on people's words to be heard."
- "You may be more comfortable building on someone else's idea, but be sure you add something of your own. For example, say, 'Joe had a good idea when he said X, but I also think doing Y would complement it.'"
- "For anyone who is shy or introverted, it is hard to talk at

meetings, but just jump in once you have an idea before you lose your confidence. As your career progresses, the egos in the room just get bigger, so get comfortable talking early."

Apprehension that a comment will not be well received may keep someone from talking, but you must learn to get over fear of rejection. It's likely you have been invited to the meeting to add value, not just to be an observer.

- "A critical part of business maturity is learning to speak up, even if all your ideas are not good ones."
- "It is better to fail for saying something wrong than for no one to notice you were there."
- "I realized the only purpose for my being on the committee was to bring my perspective. If I did not speak up, what value did I bring?"
- "Sometimes I have to remind myself that I don't care what these people think, since I am already a member of the club."
- "The healthiest demonstration of a relationship is to challenge or push back."

One concern is that you will be asked questions and may not know all the answers. While you may be worried, you cannot let it show.

- "It is important to act assured. If you get asked a question and need time, don't just sit there or people will think you are not very smart. Say, 'That's a good question' while you are thinking of the answer."
- "If you are not sure, say so firmly. For example, 'I believe the number is X, but I will check it and get back to you.'"
- "When you have done a lot of work, don't give anyone any reason to doubt your information."

Even if you are not supposed to speak, stay involved in the meeting. Act like a participant. Take notes that you can refer to later.

- "Be an active listener. Pay attention. Nod your head. People like to feel the audience understands."

- "Watch the people you admire and see what they do in meetings."

Be sure you understand the meeting etiquette. It varies by company culture and can be different if it is an internal meeting versus one involving outsiders.

- "Assess the environment. What are the spoken and unspoken rules of the place?"
- "Always be sure you know what behavior is acceptable at the meeting. Can you check emails with your computer or handheld, text-message, or take phone calls?"
- "There may be different rules on what is acceptable for senior and junior people. Sometimes senior people can get calls, but junior people are expected to turn their phones off."

Advanced technology does not always make communications easy. Complications arise when meetings are held by conference calls or using videoconferencing.

- "On conference calls it is hard to find breaks to make a point."
- "When there is a pregnant pause on the other end of the line, I do not know if that means the person is irritated or confused, because I cannot see a face."
- "Videoconferencing seems easier, but it's not. The lag makes it even harder to know when the other person is finished."

There are some simple recommendations for improving the quality of communications when everyone is not around the same table. You should anticipate problems and try to overcome them.

- "Plan a phone meeting or videoconference the same way you would an in-person meeting. Send out an agenda and the written materials in advance. Introduce all the parties before the start of the meeting."
- "Ask for feedback as you go along. Don't assume they understand or agree with what you are saying."

- "It is critical to learn to listen effectively for cues from the other side, including tone and loudness of the voices. Listening to how others react can also help you develop your own style."

Plan in advance ways to make the meeting successful, whether in person or on a conference call. Try to find out the agenda ahead of time and discuss with your boss what type of role you can play.

- "Go to the key people in advance of a meeting and ask if you can give part of a presentation. If that is not feasible, ask if you can answer any questions on your area of expertise."
- "Sometimes you can take charge and open the meeting with a simple comment such as, 'Maybe we should get started.'"
- "Think through the meeting the way you would an interview. Always have some questions or comments prepared before you walk in."

Sometimes meetings degenerate into a disorganized event, which can make it difficult to get your ideas out. Just keep focused on getting your points across.

- "Some people do a typical one-upmanship in a meeting. Just remember: the ideas that pop out in the first five minutes are generally not the best, so you do not need to be the one who starts."
- "Men have louder voices and sometimes get more actively involved in the conversation, but I believe that the person who sits quietly and makes an insightful comment is as good as someone talking all the time."

If you act like a subordinate, people will start thinking of you in that role. Be cognizant of the image you want to portray at the meeting.

- "Where you sit in a room is important. If you sit at the end of the table, no one will hear you. Sitting toward the middle is more powerful, and you can be heard."

- "Don't sit near the phone or people will expect you to answer it if it rings. If copies need to be made, call your assistant, but don't go do it yourself."

✓ **Takeaways:** Know the material to be discussed at any meeting you are attending. Be prepared to make comments, and speak early in the meeting.

Do Not Sabotage Yourself with Polite Comments

Many times people inadvertently undermine the value of their own contributions by the lead-ins to their comments. They may think they are being polite, but they are acting subservient and implying that their ideas are less important than those of others.

- "When I was in business school a professor asked a question, then called on four women and wrote down the beginning of each of the answers. Every woman started out, 'I'm not sure but . . .' or 'Everyone might not agree with me, but . . .' He pointed out to us that our language told the listeners we had no confidence in what we were about to say."
- "Women often start with a discounting statement, such as, 'This is probably not important, but . . .'"
- "It is a sign of weakness to say, 'This probably isn't right but . . .'"
- "Don't say, 'I did the best I could'; say, 'This is my best effort, and I am now looking for your input.'"
- "Don't say, 'This may be different from what everyone else says, but . . .' It is an opinion. It is supposed to be different, and no one is sure."

How you say something is also important. If you act as if you believe it, others will as well.

- "You need to project confidence and authority."
- "Don't make a statement and then raise the tone of your voice like a question at the end. You will sound very tentative."

- "Avoid sounding shrill. Try to deepen your tone and you will sound more confident."
- "I had a communications coach who told me to turn up the volume on all my communications. I now understand that if I am uncomfortable with the aggression level in the conversation, I am doing OK."

✔ **Takeaways:** State your ideas powerfully. Do not undermine your own credibility by what you perceive to be a polite introduction that makes it appear you are not confident of your opinions.

Presentations Need to Involve the Audience

There are two types of presentations: one in a conference room and the other in a large, formal setting. Most people think it is easier to present to a smaller group, but even though it may be more relaxed than a formal presentation, it still has challenges.

- "Often you are sitting at a table but presenting with slides and hard copy. While this is more comfortable and interactive, it is difficult to control the pace of the meetings and manage the participants. You need to have good facilitation skills and keep the meeting on track while allowing for some discussion."
- "You need to think about transitions as you move through your topics."
- "You need to learn to think on your feet and be able to give the presentation even if your slides or copies were not there. I often tell someone just to forget the presentation and give me a 10-minute summary. Senior people use this technique as a way to evaluate people."

Learning how to make a formal presentation in front of a large audience is a difficult but necessary business skill. Most people are not natural presenters but eventually learn how to get up in front of a large audience. It will get easier with practice.

- "A formal presentation is an unnatural act, and most people get freaked out by the thought."
- "I used to be very afraid of giving presentations, but I forced myself to learn how to do it."
- "I was in a job that required me to give formal presentations. I was afraid but got over it with the help of others."

You need to get experience giving presentations, so start small and work your way up.

- "Most bosses want their subordinates to be good presenters, so ask for opportunities in low-risk situations. Start by presenting to your team, then move up to a larger group."

You have the advantage of having seen many presentations yourself in school or work before you ever have to give one, so put yourself in the shoes of the audience and consider what you want to see and hear. Use any natural advantages you might have to capture their attention.

- "Women are especially good at telling stories, and this plays well into giving examples to make your advice come alive. By making your point with an illustration, you will achieve several things: you will improve your credibility; the information will come alive; and the audience will have more fun listening to you talk."
- "I was trained as a litigator, so I learned early that people want to be interested in what you are saying. You need to tell them why they should care and get them there quickly. By making it a story, you can connect with the audience and then judge their interest in the detail."

Every situation is different, but what suggestions do people have on how to structure a presentation to make it easier for the audience to absorb the information?

- "When putting together a presentation I think of three things: Why are we here? What am I trying to tell the audience? And, what do they need to know so they will understand my message?"

▪ "The most important line is the header. It better have the key message because I will not remember the rest."

▪ "I try to get through the formal presentation in two-thirds of the allotted time and leave the remaining one-third for Q&A. If there are not many questions and we finish early, most people will think that is great because I have respected their time."

▪ "I try not to give out copies in advance so that I can control what people are viewing."

Individuals have various strategies to get comfortable before going on stage or starting the formal part of the talk. Think of this as the business equivalent of stretching before you work out.

▪ "I always get there early and walk around the audience shaking hands. That way they already have a personal connection with me before I take the stage."

▪ "I get there early and ask people why they are coming and what they are hoping to learn. I encourage people to ask questions. Then they are not frightened of me, and I am not frightened of them."

▪ "I check the podium, lighting, computer, microphone, and figure out where I am going to stand. I make sure I have plenty of water available."

▪ "I do something in the first two to three minutes to relax, such as telling a funny story or making a light comment, but then I get into the content pretty quickly."

Delivery is very important. You have spent a lot of time on the presentation with the objective of influencing the audience. Think about the best ways to do this.

▪ "Prepare. Prepare. Prepare. Poise comes from confidence."

▪ "It is very important to be comfortable, so give the presentation the way you enjoy giving it."

- "People greatly underestimate the importance of the way you say it. You are selling yourself as much as your ideas."
- "If you are saying something slowly, in a deep-pitched voice, people will think you are saying something important."
- "Slow down and make it conversational."
- "Relax and have fun. Put the presentation in perspective. You're not developing a cure for cancer."

Stay connected with your audience. Sometimes that means asking them questions. It is not a sign of weakness. It is a sign of confidence that you want to involve them.

- "If I am not sure I have gotten my point across, I stop and get a read from the audience."
- "If you see some blank faces, don't ask, 'Am I making myself clear?' Ask a question such as, 'Can you think of an example of how this concept applies in your organization?'"

Body language is important, since it conveys your level of comfort. You also do not want people to be distracted from listening to your content.

- "In a formal presentation, body language is number one. If you are restless, people will think you are insecure."
- "Stand up and own your space. Look confident and comfortable."
- "I use a few gestures to point to the slide. I don't put both hands in my pockets and never cross my arms over my chest."
- "I had to tone it down. People used to tell me I was a 'drama queen.' I am still confident, but have reined in my gestures."
- "I had a professor who used to pace in front of the class like a caged animal. I found it very irritating."

People have different comfort zones when on a stage, and you need to figure out what works for you.

- "I don't like to be frozen in one spot, but I do not invade the territory of the audience. For example, I never walk down the center aisle, since I feel that is invading their space."
- "I normally stay at the podium but move away for Q&A."
- "I never get out of the line of sight of the audience."

What do people do wrong in formal presentations? The most common criticisms were about delivery: speed, tone, and interaction with the audience.

- "A classic mistake of inexperienced presenters is rushing through the material too quickly."
- "Women often speak too softly and cannot be heard. Remember that you need to fill up a large room."
- "There is nothing worse than someone trying to be funny when they are not. Don't use humor if it is not your natural style."
- "Some people hesitate to make eye contact."
- "Young people often talk too much. Stop when you have made your point."

There are two schools of thought on what to wear while making a formal presentation: stand out or don't draw attention to your clothes. It depends upon the audience and the impression you are trying to make. Always be sure you are comfortable in whatever you choose to wear.

- "Your physical appearance is important. You are not just there to convey information but influence the audience as well. You need to look like an authority figure."
- "Wear a solid color, navy blue or black. Wear high heels to make you taller and be more of a physical presence."
- "Wear a bright color, pink or yellow, just not black."
- "Wear black. Don't distract the audience from what you are saying."
- "Wear what makes you feel comfortable. If you like black, wear black. If you like colors, wear colors."
- "Before I decide what to wear I think about the audience and ask myself whether I want to stand out or not."

Even the best presenters felt they had benefited from professional help and recommended it for others.

- "If the company does not have presentation coaching, ask for professional help."
- "People forget that a presentation is a different form of oratory and you need formal training."
- "I needed a voice coach. He taught me not to use a monotone."

✔ **Takeaways:** Tailor your presentation to the audience and make it worth people's time. Know your material and your confidence will come across. Wear a professional outfit that reflects your style and considers what is appropriate for the audience. If you are presenting in a small group, the same rules apply. Be comfortable enough to give a summary without going through your presentation.

■ Career-Enhancing Moves

1. Get to the point quickly in your written and verbal communications.
2. Proofread all written communications, including emails.
3. Be well prepared for every meeting.
4. Speak in the first half of any meeting you attend, if people at your level are speaking.
5. Plan a phone conversation the way you would a meeting.
6. Get formal presentation training.

■ Career-Limiting Moves

1. Do not undermine your contribution with a self-denigrating lead-in.
2. Do not use email or voice mail for sensitive or personal information that you would not like others to see or hear.

Four

Interactions at Work: Bosses, Peers, Clients, Administrative Staff, and Significant Others

My first assignment as an associate at a major investment bank was working on a team headed by a vice president. His counsel to me seemed harsh at the time, but in retrospect it was probably the best business advice I ever received: "The people who love you are not in this building." This chapter will talk about interactions between people at different levels at work and why the work relationships you develop are critical to your success.

Companies Have Distinct Cultures

There are many definitions of the word *culture*, but in a business context it refers to the way people treat each other, what they value, and how the work is accomplished. Culture is the business equivalent of personality. You will get an idea of the company culture from its mission statement, generally available on the Web site, but sometimes there is a disconnect between the vision and reality.

During the interview process, you should ask people about the culture. In most companies, people can describe the culture in a few sentences. If you have done your homework and understand the culture of the firm before joining, fitting in should not be difficult.

- "Make sure you understand what they value and make sure you value it, too."
- "Trust your instinct about people when you are interviewing."
- "Understand the general climate of the organization."
- "You are going to spend a lot of time with these people, so make sure you will enjoy working with them."

Your company's culture will significantly influence the personal style you develop for work. Some companies place a high value on consensus building, while others foster a more aggressive style. Certain work environments expect long hours regardless of the level of work, while others encourage people to leave at 5:00 PM if their work is done. Different people thrive in different environments, so it is all a matter of fit.

- "The language here is 'work with' not 'work for.'"
- "Clearly there are moments of hierarchy around pay and promotion, but in doing the work we want it as flat as possible."
- "Figure out how much face time is needed. How political is the organization?"
- "In most financial services firms, there is strong internal competition, but people expect that."

Everyone agrees you need to be comfortable where you work, but that means picking the right company, not trying to change the organization to fit your personality.

- "Everyone needs to conform and adapt a little to the business environment. Just find a place where you do not have to make too many changes."
- "If your style is to be open and warm, then continue to be that way at work. If you have to hide who you are, you will not be productive."
- "You can be a member of the team, but do not forget who you are."

✔ **Takeaways:** Before you join an organization make sure you understand the company culture and how people work together. You need to find the right company for your personality. Do not expect a company to change to fit your behavior.

The "Work" You

The way you interact with people determines the impression you make on them, how they perceive you, and how much they will support you. In your personal life, your family and friends care about you and are willing to give you the benefit of the doubt if you do something that they think is inappropriate. In business, however, the standards are higher.

- "I tell new people that no matter how hard we try to create a great atmosphere, this is not your family, this is business."

Remember when you join a firm that your plan is usually to move up in the organization, so you need to create an image that is suited for higher-level assignments, not just the work you are doing now. Even if you only plan on being there for a short time, you will want a good recommendation from your current employer.

When you join any organization, you need to observe the senior people carefully and see how they act. This should help determine your work style. The open-book, casual attitude that a junior person may come in with can be totally inappropriate if you would like to move up to a more senior role. No one is suggesting you merely act out a part at work. However, everyone has multiple facets to her personality and you want to emphasize your professional qualities in the beginning.

- "Behave as if you held the position you want to hold."
- "It is imperative to be perceived as a professional."
- "A lot of your success in moving up in the ranks depends on figuring out what is the right thing to do in your firm. The people and the place determine the acceptable behavior."

You will learn over time what works at your company, so don't rush in. You need to decide how much personal detail you should reveal to your work colleagues. Don't mistake professional courtesy for friendship, which takes a much longer time to develop.

- "When starting out in business, listen more than you talk. Don't start sharing a lot of information right away. Ask people about themselves, and take cues from them on what they would like to discuss."
- "In a friendly organization young people think they can jump-start a professional relationship with a personal one, but they cannot. The normal sequence is to develop your professional relationship with someone first and then a personal one. If you try to flip it around people will be uncomfortable."

What people discuss in casual conversation depends on the company. Again, the smart thing to do is to listen first before you do a lot of talking. Recognize that you may need to change your style when you change companies.

- "What do the successful people in your company talk about? Families, children, sports? Follow their lead on the subjects discussed."
- "Professional communications can cross into an appropriate friendly conversation about family and vacations. You just don't need to get into too much detail."
- "When I was in a law firm, I could be a 'lone ranger.' In a company, however, I need to work collaboratively with other people, and I found they like knowing a little bit about me."
- "At one company I discovered a few other people who loved to read. Not only did we have great discussions, but I got a lot of wonderful reading suggestions."
- "Don't say anything that undercuts your professionalism. It is so important to be respected."

There are times when your manager needs to know personal information that might impact your work or time you may need to take off to tend to personal issues. Also, when you are new to town, your colleagues may the best source of references for things you need in your personal life.

- "A young woman who worked for me ended up in the emergency room over the weekend, so my standard 'How was your weekend?' got a different response than I expected. It turned out she needed a cardiologist but was new to town and did not even have a primary care physician. I was able to find her an excellent doctor and get her an appointment right away."
- "I don't want to know if someone had a fight with her boyfriend, but if her father had a heart attack and she wants to go see him, I want to be sure we get her the coverage she needs."

Women tend to be more open than men about their personal lives, and there are both positives and negatives to this approach. Many women said they had found that their ability to connect with people had been an asset in their careers, both within their own company and in building client relationships.

- "Real relationships are about building bridges, and women are great at that."
- "Women have more substantial relationships with clients and colleagues than men do."
- "Creating a bond with colleagues and clients is a strength many women possess. The issue is how to create this bond without diminishing your professional demeanor."

Many believe that women disclose too many personal details, and most have struggled to find the right balance of being both friendly and professional.

- "When women are forging a relationship with someone, they try to make the person comfortable and end up talking too much and revealing too much personal information."
- "I have seen two extremes. On one end of the spectrum is the woman with no control over what she says, and on the other end is the one who is very uptight and never reveals anything about herself. Neither is successful."

- "Early in my career I erred on the side of being too self-contained. I was told I needed to open up more so that people felt more comfortable with me as a member of the team."
- "This is not Oprah. Don't get to that level of detail too quickly."

✓ **Takeaways:** Be yourself, but be cautious about revealing too much personal information at work until you feel out the culture of the organization. You can always tell people more about yourself, but you cannot take back a personal comment once it has been spoken.

Your Boss Is Your Most Important Client

The person you report to is the person who will have the most impact on your career in your early years. Most people confess it took them awhile to realize this and wish they had figured it out sooner. Do what your boss needs first and always make her look good. The *American Heritage Dictionary* defines a client as "one for whom professional services are rendered." That sounds like a good description of a boss as well, and a number of people picked up on this theme.

- "Treat your boss as if he or she were a client, and you will seldom make a mistake."
- "For a young person, the most important client is the person you report to."
- "I tell young people to always do what the boss wants first. We often lose sight of that simple rule and follow our own priorities."
- "Try to make your boss's life easier. For example, when a boss asked for names of people on the team so that he could send a thank-you note, I not only sent the names, but drafted the note and copied his assistant to be sure it got done."
- "In professional service firms you may have many bosses, which makes it more complicated. Each project is an op-

portunity for a new impression. That is both good news and bad news."

- "Make your boss look good by helping him get his tasks accomplished."
- "At the end of the day your boss is the one who will evaluate you, so do not reveal anything that could be viewed as a weakness."

While everyone agrees that the boss is important, there seems to be a range of advice on how to treat him or her. Several executives said junior people do not always understand that the boss is always the boss. You need to respect that line. A lot will depend on the individuals involved.

- "A relationship with the boss needs to grow over time."
- "Follow the boss's lead on what type of relationship she or he wants to have."
- "We bosses send out a confusing message. I am nice and friendly, but people don't always realize they need to earn the right to be my friend."
- "There is a certain line you do not cross with the boss. Bosses do not appreciate it when you try to get too close."
- "Don't ever try to use the personal rapport you have developed with your boss as an excuse for not getting your job done. You might think your 'friendly' boss will 'understand' if you go home because you are tired, but your boss only cares that the work is not getting done."
- "It is always awkward to socialize with the boss."
- "Screen things out before you talk to your boss. Be more guarded."

Don't just assume that the most senior person is the only one you need to impress. There are often several people more senior between you and your official boss.

- "Young people act more entitled over time, and some are disrespectful of middle-level managers. This is not healthy for the organization and we will not tolerate it, since it

will lead to anarchy. Those middle-level managers have
important things to teach the junior people."

- "The senior people don't like it when there is no respect for
  hierarchy."
- "It is hard to figure out the nuances of looking up and
  looking down."

Most bosses will appreciate professional input from younger colleagues. Remember that they hired you to be part of a team.

- "Bosses look for people to be honest. Don't just tell them
  what you think they want to hear. Tell the boss your ideas
  and give real opinions."
- "I love it when people push me on an issue."
- "I started making suggestions to my boss about the business and managing people, and he started using me as a
  sounding board. I never got any credit, but he was thrilled
  with my ideas."

Be very careful about any office politics you try to play that involve
your boss.

- "It is a big mistake to try to go around or above your boss
  if you disagree on something or just want more exposure.
  You will get a bad reputation, and no one will want you
  working for them."
- "A woman working for me went to my boss and said I was
  not doing my job, which was not true. My boss thought I
  would not be able to get rid of her since the woman and I
  were friends, but I fired her for insubordination."

One point several people raised: never act flirtatious with your boss.

- "Women need to be very careful that that things they think
  of as 'friendly' are not perceived as 'flirtatious.'"
- "I was in a job where I traveled a lot with my boss, and
  I started teasing him about things that were his personal
  likes or dislikes I had observed on the road. However, to

other people my teasing implied we had a more intimate relationship than we did, and he did not appreciate it."

Try to remember that the boss is human and needs positive feedback like everyone else.

- "The other night our boss took a group of us out to dinner, and a couple of days later he mentioned that no one had thanked him. I thought of it as a company event but then realized he had arranged it and given up his evening and expected to be thanked, just as in any social situation."

✔ **Takeaways:** Treat your boss very carefully. Be friendly, but maintain a professional distance. Make sure your work priorities are the boss's work priorities.

All Peers Are Not Equal

Many people assume that their work peers will be their best friends, but this is not always true. While you may like the people you work with, and have a more relaxed relationship with them than you do with your boss, keep in mind that there are many levels of friendship. For example, you are probably closer to your sister and share more things with her than your next-door neighbor, with whom you are also friendly. Similarly, only a small subset of peers you meet during your career will become lifelong friends. That is not to say that you cannot have excellent working relationships with people; you just need to think of these relationships in the overall context of the business world. Peers are both competitors for future job assignments and potential supervisors down the road.

- "It is fine to have friends, but remember they are colleagues and not necessarily best friends."
- "Think of the people sitting around you as teammates. You are working together, but you are all competing for positions on the team."

It is a complicated equation dealing with peers because while you may know they are potential competitors, you are inclined to like them. You also need to demonstrate the ability to work well with others to get ahead.

- "We prize the ability to work in a team."
- "Here people get promoted more often if they are seen as 'glue' to an organization."

Before you share detailed personal information or controversial opinions with peers, be sure you know them well, because this information could be used against you in the future. This does not mean everyone is out to "get you," but the old adage of "better safe than sorry" is something to consider when developing peer relationships. Sometimes people think they are helping you when they use information you told them in confidence.

- "You need to have friends. You can't survive in a political office environment without someone to talk to who understands the background, but be very careful what you confide to people."
- "Sometimes you need to blow off steam, but it should be carefully thought through. The best thing is to use people outside work for that."
- "Don't reveal anxieties about your career, how you are getting along with the boss, or anything negative about the work environment."
- "You had better know the people you are talking to and know how much you can trust them."
- "A close friend at work 'neglected' to tell me about a great job opening because she thought it would be too stressful for me given some problems I was having at home."

People from diverse industries and companies had different stories on how they interacted with peers, showing again that the culture of the company can dictate what is considered normal.

- "Peers have always been the people I have opened up to. They give me advice and provide a noncompetitive support network."
- "You need to choose with whom you confide very carefully, but the fun part about having colleagues is that you can share things no one outside the office would understand."
- "You share a lot of work and challenges, so you form a common bond."
- "In the 'alpha male' culture I am in, revealing anything about your personal life eats into your credibility as a professional."

As you progress in your career, the nature of your relationship with your peers changes. Even if you are in an organization where there are "classes" that come in every year, people tend to move into different areas of the firm and the original tight-knit group becomes a loose network.

- "When you are younger, you are very friendly with your peers, often socialize with them, and it's very collegial. As you advance, distinctions are made and people become less forthcoming."
- "You will end up building alliances with people who can help you, but be very selective. Some people will suck information from you and use it against you."
- "Don't avoid competition with your friends at work."

Sometimes you find yourself in an environment where you are the odd person out and you need to find ways to bridge the distance between you and your peers. This can take time and patience. Many of the examples below are based on gender, but anyone from another part of the country or with different schooling can feel excluded.

- "I work in an industry that is a closed club of white men who went to the same prep schools and colleges. I had to figure out how to break into the club without driving them

crazy. It was a subtle dance. Over time I grew to have their trust and respect, and they started to include me."
- "Don't wait to be invited if the group is going out. Just get up and go with them. Assume you are included."
- "Women don't spend enough time with the guys. You need to go in and just shoot the shit. Have three or four general-interest topics such as business news, strategic issues, or what is going on with the competition."

You are inevitably going to have peers with whom there is mutual dislike. Senior people will judge you on how well you can work with others, so do not waste any time trying to convince your boss or office-mates that she or he is a bad person. You need to put aside your differences and figure out how to work together with minimum friction.

- "One of my worst career mistakes was a long-standing feud with a guy I couldn't stand. I thought he was arrogant and misled people into thinking he was a lot smarter than he was. I got branded as 'not a team player,' since I was so vocal in my complaints about him."
- "Don't become obsessed with what your peers are doing. Don't compare yourself. Do your personal best."
- "Get used to the fact that not everyone is going to like you."
- "One woman who works for me is paranoid that some people are out to get her. It really detracts from the way I see her."

Again there is the caution about sending out signals to your peers that could be misinterpreted as pursuing more than a business relationship.

- "Single women need to be careful that what they think of as being 'friendly' is not perceived by others as 'flirtatious.'"
- "Don't think of your coworkers as potential spouses. Think of them as people who are going to work for you in the future."

Many advise not letting your company become the center of your social life. You can be friendly and go out with groups after work, but if you only see people from work it can cause you to lose perspective about whether the company is the best place for you.

- "It is hard for people who move from out of town to meet people outside of work, but it is dangerous to build your social structure around work."
- "You need a social circle where you can just be yourself and not worry about what you say."
- "Don't pick roommates who work in your department, or better yet, share an apartment with someone from another company. Roommate tensions get magnified when you work together."
- "A woman I know was let go in a downsizing, and all her old work friends shunned her as if being fired was contagious."

✔ **Takeaways:** You will develop some close relationships at work, but go slowly and be cautious what you share. Your peer today may be your supervisor or subordinate tomorrow. Teamwork is important and you need to build strong working relationships, but these will not always develop into deep friendships.

Clients Need to Be Cultivated

Everyone has clients. If you are in a line job, your clients will be outside the firm. If you are in a support role, your clients are inside your own company. In a professional service business, the first fork in the road is whether you are comfortable dealing directly with clients or prefer to be a person who works on business that others bring in. Being a specialist can be an excellent career, but in many organizations the people who "originate" the business get paid more and have more power than people who "execute" the business.

- "In law firms, you only ultimately get promoted if you bring in clients."

If your plan is to be someone who generates business, you need to start early in your career developing the skills needed to impress people who are often older and have been in business a lot longer. You may have the advantage of excellent technical skills, but unless the potential client recognizes those skills and feels comfortable relying on your advice for a major transaction, he or she will not hire your firm. Your goal is to become a trusted adviser, which is going to take time.

- "In a client service business you need to be assertive in developing client relationships. Do not assume it will just happen."
- "I have older clients and I want them to think, 'That woman is smart.'"
- "What do you want the client to think of you? I want him or her to think of me as an equal in ideas."

It is difficult to develop relationships with clients, many of whom are older than you when you start your career. The general consensus is to stick to "safe" discussion topics when you do not know a person well: business, current events, sports, and the latest technology in cars or electronics.

General business news or the client's company is always a good place to start. Before you can talk knowledgeably, however, you're going to need to do some studying.

- "I tell every young person to read *The Wall Street Journal* and the business section of the local paper. Even if you are busy, read the front page of every section of *The Journal*."
- "If you have specific clients, get on the email list for press releases so that you stay current on their business and can ask them about a new customer or product."
- "Make a business-oriented Web site your home page so that every time you log on to the Internet you catch the latest business news."
- "If you work with companies in New York, check *The New York Times* every day."
- "Ask clients about their business: what is going well and

what the new projects are. Not only does it help you to know your clients and their business better, it lets people know you are interested and allows you to 'sell' any products or services your firm has that can help them."

- "Young people are often not comfortable talking to older people about business. I ask them what their parents do and if either parent is in business, I tell them to pick one business topic from the paper and call the business parent once a week and discuss it. If there are no parents in business, ask a family friend."

You may not be a sports person, but you need to know the basics or you will be left out of a lot of conversations. However, do not carry on a long discussion on a sport you do not know much about. You just need to know enough to ask a few intelligent questions and let the other person do the talking.

- "Even if you are not a big sports fan, read the front page of the sports section. Know the major news in the sports world."
- "When a client's team is in the playoffs, I email him after each game. It just gets a little competitive when his team is playing mine!"

Many people keep apprised of the latest and greatest, whether it is in cars, cameras, cell phones, or other devices.

- "Ask her what she thought of the article in the paper on the new cars."
- "Compliment him on his new cell phone or PDA, and ask him what he likes about it."

Sometimes the hardest part is just starting the conversation with someone when it appears you have little in common. They are probably just as uncomfortable as you are, but one of you has to start talking first, so jump in and you will almost always find something in common.

- "You need to learn to deal with people very different than yourself. Success depends on building a relationship."
- "You have to get past the stereotypes."

Be careful asking about family until you know someone well. While most people like talking about their family, a client may have some family issues that he or she does not want to discuss with you. If family topics come up, don't volunteer comments that align you with the children. It is key that the client relates to you as an equal and does not think of you as a "child." People rarely seek business advice from their children.

✔ **Takeaways:** Treat your clients very professionally and develop topics of conversation to help build a relationship. Get to know your client's business well. Your goals are to be trusted and treated as a valued adviser.

How to Get the Administrative Staff to Support You

One of the most difficult things to learn when you join an organization is how to effectively use the administrative staff, whose importance junior people often underestimate. The administrative staff can impact both your effectiveness and your reputation within the company. The relationship with an assistant can be one of the most complicated relationships to manage in business, and many had stories of things either they had done wrong themselves or had seen others do badly.

- "Administrative staff will make you or break you."
- "The staff has their own network, and they are very plugged into what is going on. Whether you treat them well or poorly, it will get around and you'll have a reputation one way or the other."

Your assistant is there to provide leverage for you. You need to plan ahead to use his or her time effectively and not create a crisis when better planning could have avoided a problem.

- "I meet at the beginning of the week with my assistant and tell her what my schedule is, what I need done, how she can help me, and what my priorities are."
- "If you use your assistant to off-load some of your work, you will be more productive."
- "Know what you can delegate and what you cannot delegate. If a person is experienced, off-load as much as possible. Trust her to do the job you hired her to do."
- "Be direct and specific enough to guide someone, but don't tell the person how to get the job done."

Not everyone feels comfortable asking for help, but you need to learn to delegate. Managing someone else's time is a new skill to be learned when starting out in business. Think of it as the first step in developing leadership skills.

- "Some young people are intimidated by the fact that someone is working for them. You have authority and need to learn how to use it properly."
- "You have to get over asking the administrative staff to do things."
- "Don't act as if everything your assistant does is a favor for you. If you do, the assistant will reciprocate and act as if she is doing you a favor."
- "Early in my career, when I could not get support I did the work myself. This kept me from getting other work done and got me in trouble with my boss."
- "Many people who have played sports are very comfortable handing things off, since they played on teams and understand interdependency."

In most companies, administrative support is shared among a number of people and one issue is how the junior person gets the support she needs.

- "Ask your assistant if she is overwhelmed. Work with the other person or people she is supporting and discuss the situation if there are too many 'rush' jobs."
- "If you are not getting the support you need, don't take

it out on your assistant. Talk to the person causing the bottleneck."

- "If your relationship with your assistant is not working, tell your boss you are having problems getting the work done. Do not personalize it, but get a new assistant."
- "If you need a new assistant, be sure the reason is understood by your boss. If you change assistants often, people will assume you are the problem."

For many people the difficult question was what type of personal relationship to have with the administrative staff, especially early in a career when the professional is young and has little authority and the assistant often is older and more experienced. The problem of young professionals learning to work with people who have more practical experience is not unique to business. Television shows are full of stories of seasoned nurses who have to put up with a new group of young doctors every year.

- "Be polite and friendly, but do not get confused about who is senior."
- "It is a complicated message. On the one hand, I will roll up my sleeves and work with you. On the other hand, I am senior to you."
- "Some young people who are not sure of their status tend to act more overbearing than necessary."
- "If you communicate to your assistant that you will be an advocate, you will have fewer issues."
- "They do not have to like you, but they have to respect you."

Relationships I heard about tended to be at one extreme or another. Some prefer a more distant professional relationship and recommended it for others. Other people are very close to their assistants and it works well for them. As with most human interaction, it will be influenced by the personalities of the two people involved.

- "Young women can be friendly with administrative staff and get very close, but this is a 'watch out.' The problem is that this type of relationship may impact how senior people see a young woman. She might be viewed as part of the administrative staff rather than as a junior professional."

- "If you are too friendly with the administrative staff, you will not be perceived as a 'player.'"
- "I once had an assistant who wanted to know every detail of my personal life and wanted me to know every detail of hers. Every day she wanted to catch up. It was draining and time-consuming. I swore I'd never get into that type of relationship again, and I haven't. I am now much more private."
- "My assistant is my friend. She takes care of me and I take care of her."
- "I consider my assistant to be a confidante in certain areas, but I draw the line at talking about senior people with her."

Good relationships with administrative staff, both within your own firm and at clients' firms, can be very beneficial. These people not only can help you get your job done, they can get you access to senior people.

- "Your boss's assistant is his right-hand person. Her impression of you will impact the boss's opinion."
- "I was in sales for a long time and learned that unless I developed a rapport with the client's administrative people, I could never get through."
- "When there is a crunch and we need people to work late, I can always get someone to work for me, but other people have trouble. For them, no one ever seems to be able to stay late."
- "Earlier in my career I worked with the woman who is now the assistant for the chief executive officer. We have a great relationship, and she always makes sure I get right through to him."

Women spoke of difficulties they had encountered with assistants in being taken seriously as a professional. If this is happening to you, talk to your assistant. If it continues, get a new assistant.

- "It turned out an assistant I had for years was answering my phone with just my first name while she answered my peer's phone as 'Mr.' When I asked her about this, she said she never thought about it. When I pointed out that using my first name made me sound less professional, she acted surprised."
- "There was an assistant in our firm who did not want to work for female professionals. She had observed (correctly) that more men than women progressed to the partner level. Since she thought her job security and pay level depended on the progress of her boss, she preferred to place her bet on a man."

People pointed out that in many companies there is no upward mobility from an administrative position. Since assistants receive little benefit from working long hours, they expect a better working environment than a professional with the opportunity to move up. Many just want to be appreciated for the work they do, even if there is no mobility.

- "Don't ask people to stay late because you did a poor job planning. They have a life outside of work."
- "Remember to say thank you."

✔️ **Takeaways:** Your assistant is a professional. Use her or him effectively to leverage your time. If you cannot develop a good working relationship, ask for a different assistant.

Spouses and Significant Others Can Impact Your Career

There is a great variation by company on how often you will see the spouses and significant others of your colleagues. At some firms, there are regular social events that involve family members, and at other companies, you only meet spouses if they happen to drop by the office. Never assume your spouse or significant other is invited to a company event. If it is not clear, ask.

- "I learned quickly that the business social event really is an oxymoron."

If you are bringing your spouse or significant other to a company event, be sure you have a conversation in advance about what you would like to accomplish and how he can help you. Remember that while this is a social event there will be people present who can impact your career, so provide a good briefing. While it may seem unfair, people will be forming an opinion of your guest, just as you will be forming an opinion of theirs. Remind your spouse or significant other of important people's names, and provide some background information on them. Ask your spouse to:

- Be friendly but not reveal too much personal information.
- Refrain from telling any stories about you.
- Not talk about any company business you may have discussed at home.
- Avoid public displays of affection other than taking a hand or arm as you are coming or going.
- Keep away from controversial subjects such as politics or religion.
- Drink moderately or not at all.
- Watch for your cues on when you want to leave.

The way you interact with the spouses of your colleagues will be important to your career. There will likely be a discussion about you after the event, so be careful what you say and do.

- "Don't underestimate the value of a professional, articulate conversation with the spouse of the boss. It is highly likely he or she uses the spouse as a sounding board."
- "Treat a spouse as a client. Chances are a spouse knows a lot about you already."
- "Don't avoid them. Introduce yourself."

In order to make a personal connection with the spouse you need to find a way to have a good conversation with her or him. There will always be something you can talk about: family, children, pets, movies, charities. You just may need to work to find common interests.

- "If you can, find out something about her in advance so that you know what interests her."
- "When I was young, the first question I asked was 'What do you do?' and older stay-at-home moms often felt put on the defensive. I now look for a neutral topic, asking about something in the newspaper or vacation plans."
- "Treat spouses respectfully. Get to know them."
- "Talk about your hobbies and interests, and ask them about theirs."

A potential problem for a young woman is that the spouses may not like the idea of their husbands working with you. A particular concern seemed to be when young women travel with married men.

- "Be extraordinarily careful how you treat a man in front of his wife. A wife will be looking at how you interact with her husband and her antennae will be up."
- "People work such long hours in their jobs that it is likely you spend more waking hours with her husband than she does."
- "Many women do not like their husbands traveling with young, attractive women. If there is ever a time to reveal something personal, this is it. Tell her how happy you are with your husband or boyfriend. You do not want her to be fearful or anxious about your relationship with her husband."

✓ **Takeaways:** The spouse of the boss will be judging you, so have a good conversation with her or him since the spouse is likely your boss's confidante. Make a connection with the female spouses to be sure they realize you are not a threat to them. If you have a husband or significant other, provide a briefing before any company event on what you want to accomplish.

■ Career-Enhancing Moves

1. Create a professional image. Be friendly, but do not reveal too much personal information.
2. Treat your boss like a client. Make sure your boss's work takes priority over everything else. It is your job to make him or her look good.
3. Go slowly on developing deep friendships with peers. A peer today could be a supervisor or subordinate tomorrow.
4. Have a good but professional relationship with the administrative staff and leverage their time effectively. They can make you or break you.
5. Build relationships with clients. Your goal is to be a trusted adviser.
6. Treat your boss's spouse respectfully. A spouse is likely to be the boss's closest confidante.

■ Career-Limiting Moves

1. Do not put your own work in front of something your boss has asked you to do.
2. Do not lay out all your problems to your colleagues. Find another place to vent your frustrations.

Five

Building Bridges Inside and Outside the Company: Task Forces, Leadership, Networking, and Mentors

Think of your career as a product that needs to be designed (managing your career), manufactured (doing your job well and working hard), and marketed (making sure people know your value). To perfect the product, you need to test it out in a number of markets and with different consumers. Your boss and department are just too narrow a place to get all the feedback and skills you need to move ahead. Let's look at some ways for you to get smarter and work on that product: your career.

Task Forces, Committees, and Projects

Task forces, committees, and other short-term projects are excellent ways to get exposure to different parts of the business and meet people who might be good contacts for you in the future. They also help you learn skills that may not be necessary in your current job but would be useful for other opportunities. The problem is that these activities take away from your "day job," so you need to balance time spent getting exposure versus maintaining your performance at a high level.

How do you decide which committees would be good for you, and how do you get these assignments? It depends on the company and what is considered important in that culture. If you do not get on a standing committee at first, keep trying.

- "Only join a task force if it is well defined, is likely to succeed, has a good sponsor, visibility, and there are people on the task force you want to meet."
- "In big companies it may be better for you to be on a large task force where you do less but have more visibility. In

a smaller company, you might be able to get a leadership position on at least part of the project."

- "I looked for projects or committees focused on issues that impacted the bottom line: cost reduction, quality, and organizational effectiveness."
- "Your boss must be supportive of putting you on the task force or it will never work."
- "Getting on a task force is seen as a positive thing, especially in a matrixed organization. It implies you are trying to help improve the company."
- "In our firm recruiting is key, so we only let our best people recruit and rotate the people every year."

Some people were reluctant to be on certain committees, since they felt these assignments might hurt a career more than help it. Notice that recruiting was mentioned above by one person as critical, but others below felt it was a waste of time. It all depends on what is important in the company.

- "Pick how you use your committee time. Don't go for a touchy-feely committee like hiring. Go for something more economically driven."
- "Don't get pigeonholed into support projects such as training or recruiting."
- "I had mixed feelings about being on a diversity committee. I did not want to be seen as a one-issue person."

There were even some people who felt all these extracurricular activities were a waste of time. It should be noted that this group was definitely in the minority, but it is a useful perspective, especially if your boss is in this category.

- "If you are in a line job, only the numbers matter. Don't help plan events. Don't do marketing materials. Don't recruit on campus. Focus on your numbers. At the end of the year, that's all that counts."

✔ **Takeaways:** Get on a well-defined task force with people you want to meet and where you can develop new skills. Be sure to keep up your regular work and that your boss supports your being part of the project.

Developing Leadership Presence

Why do you need to be a leader? Can't you get ahead by just doing something well? Maybe the answer is yes if you want to stay in one narrow place, but to move upward in a career, you need to develop what a chief executive officer once described to me as "leadership presence." When you think of the word leader you may think it only applies to CEOs or heads of major divisions, but note the definition of leadership in the Army leadership manual provided below. This is a broad definition and if you added the word *company* before mission, it could be in an employee training class:

> Leadership is *influencing* people—by providing purpose, direction, and motivation—while *operating* to accomplish the mission and *improving* the organization.

The executives were loath to define a leader, since they had all worked with many types of leaders, and various organizations respond to different leadership styles. The feeling was that leaders develop over time, and are molded both by their own personalities and the circumstances in which they find themselves.

- "There are many kinds of leaders. Each person's path to becoming a leader is unique."

However, people spoke about some of their own ideal leadership characteristics.

- "Leaders have an affinity to be with people, the power of a positive personality, and enormous integrity."
- "I think a leader is someone who creates a climate where people are comfortable questioning the status quo."

- "Leaders need to be great managers, smart, and use a confident, assertive speaking style to express their views."
- "Leaders have good judgment and use it, are true to their core values, and don't compromise."
- "People have your number. They like to follow leaders with unimpeachable integrity who really care."

Many people used the word *integrity* when defining a leader, but only one person went on to define integrity in a day-to-day office environment.

- "Having integrity doesn't just mean you do not lie or steal. It means being honest with the people you work with, saying 'I forgot to do it,' rather than 'I could not find anything.' Telling someone 'I don't know' is fine and has credibility."

Everyone develops a personal leadership style that builds on his or her own strengths.

- "I build family-like teams that have a strong allegiance to the team. People who work for me go above and beyond what is required and look out for each other."
- "My own management style is more collaborative and less hierarchical than others. I want people to understand why they are doing something."
- "I do not like the command-and-control model. I like to put issues on the table for discussion. I still make decisions but after input from others. It may take longer, but the people around the table are involved and in the end it is more productive."
- "Look at what inspires you. That is what will feel authentic to you. At the end of the day, you need to be yourself."
- "Build a leadership style that plays up to your natural strengths."

Don't be intimidated about learning leadership skills. The consensus was that leaders are developed over time, so if you are not comfortable being a leader today, it does not mean you cannot become a leader in the future.

- "Leaders are just people. They are not any smarter than you or any tougher. Maybe the differences are all in your head. Just stop worrying about becoming a leader and see how it goes."
- "Anyone can be a leader if you work on the right recipe."
- "You can lead an army as long as you are fair, honest, and open. People will want to grow with you."
- "You can be trained to avoid obvious leadership mistakes."
- "If you are not perceived as being a leader, try to find out why."

What suggestions did people have that you can control? One easy suggestion is your personal style.

- "Self-confidence is key. Project an image of capability and substance."
- "You can't discount your overall manner: voice, composure, appropriate language, dress. Do you look and sound like a leader?"
- "Body language is very important. Do you look like someone who gives orders or takes orders?"
- "Own a room when you walk into it. You want to project an image that says, 'All of you people need me.'"
- "Start every meeting with a professional handshake and the exchange of business cards. Stand up straight, make eye contact, be a presence in the room. When you get down to business, don't apologize when you speak. You must have an opinion and be prepared to take risk."

What are some early ways to develop leadership skills? Look at everything as a leadership opportunity, and get training if you can.

- "When you are given a project to lead, get good people on your team, get the project done, make sure everyone has a positive experience, and get through any roadblocks. Build a positive track record."

- "If you're managing more junior people, be sure you do not increase pressure on them. Our firm is very sensitive to people who push blame and workload on others."
- "If you have the ambition to be a leader, don't be afraid, start today. There is a misconception that you can't do anything without a title, but if something needs to be improved, do what you can. You can make a difference."
- "Look for opportunities to represent your group in a meeting or presentation."
- "Try out leadership in other organizations you are involved in: industry associations, alumni groups, charities, or religious groups."
- "If you are in a supervisory role, care about the people around you."
- "Take a leadership course, even if you have to pay for it yourself."
- "There are many good leadership books out there. Read some."

The harder skills to develop revolve around building up credibility in the workplace and being very good at your job.

- "To be a leader, people need to follow you, so you need to be good at what you do and be right 95 percent of the time."
- "You need to be organized, able to get information from others, and good at setting the direction of the team. You must also be a good communicator who can get people to rally around a cause and follow you."
- "People think that the higher you go, you can just manage from 30,000 feet, but that is not true. If you want respect, you need to understand the details of complex issues to help your team."
- "You need to be assertive and be able to influence people. Have some backbone, and when you disagree with people, counter with your own data. Be open to new ideas."

- "You need to be able to establish a vision, but also make tough calls."

✓ **Takeaways:** To become a leader you must develop a presence that projects confidence in yourself. Be very good at what you do, communicate your ideas well, and take care of the people on your team.

Networking Is about Creating a Social Net

What exactly is networking? It is about making connections: both personal and professional.

- "Networking is about cultivating relationships."
- "Networking is not about who can help you. It's about who you can help. It will come back to you."
- "You must be prepared to do people favors. There is a quid pro quo in relationships."

Networking is the "in" thing, but how useful is it really to your career? Most people think it is very important for a variety of reasons.

- "Even if you like your job, you need to network for career planning. Make time for networking events even when you think you do not have the time."
- "The first year or so in a job you should just focus on your job and not try to network. However, don't wait much longer than that to get involved."
- "You need to network with people in your own firm in a professional services environment to develop internal business referrals."
- "The best advice I got was never to leave a networking event without the names of two other people to talk to. That is how I got my job."

Where is the best place to find good networks? Are there places to avoid? In order to keep your attention, you need to find groups where there is a common interest.

- "You need to find a network of people where you have a real connection. I am not a big proponent of exchanging business cards with people I do not want to know."
- "I like to be involved in professional organizations, since I know we all have the same interests."
- "Networking is critical, but be extremely careful how you spend your time. Get rid of the chaff. Go for the gold."
- "Start your own network. Introduce people you think would enjoy meeting each other. If you help them, they are more likely to help you."
- "The mistake people make is not networking outside the company. If you change jobs, you lose your entire network."
- "Make time for some networks, even if it is just your school alumni group. If you cannot go to a lot of meetings, stay in touch by email."

There were mixed opinions about the value of women's networks. The best strategy is probably to try a woman's group, but do not make this your only network.

- "I am a big believer in women's networks. After the first five years it starts to get lonely, and other people can help put things in perspective."
- "There is an automatic feeling when you are with a group of women that you can just exhale. You are with your tribe."
- "Don't network just with women."

For many people, they could network and achieve great personal satisfaction at the same time. You may not think of charities or employee activities at your firm as networking opportunities, but they are.

- "The best networks are places where you can combine business and pleasure."
- "At big companies there are lots of ways to network. There are company-sponsored events, sports teams, bands, and community service. Get out there. You will meet a lot of nice people from other communities within your firm and have fun."

- "Charitable organizations are a great place to network with people from different organizations and different fields. Try to get on a charity board."
- "Pro bono work is a great way to meet people and add real value."
- "Take a course at night."
- "Get involved in the religious organization to which you belong."

Some large companies have taken networking into their own hands and set up formal networking programs.

- "There are affinity networks in our company. Management has mixed feelings about them, but the participants find them very helpful."
- "My boss told me I should go to the company networking events, but I find them very uncomfortable."

Some people find it very difficult to walk into a room where everyone seems to know someone except you. Suddenly you feel as if you are back in middle school at a mixer, and you are the only person not dancing. Relax. Learning how to "work a room" is just another business skill you need to acquire. Have business cards handy so that you can easily get at them. Everyone has her own way of managing an event, but here are a few.

- Get a soda, but skip the food since it is impossible to carry two things and shake hands. The line at the bar is a good place to start meeting people.
- Have a sentence ready that you can use when you walk up to a person who is alone, such as, "How are you connected to the organization?" or "What did you think of the speaker?" Always introduce yourself and tell the person where you work. When joining a group already formed, stand at the edge of the circle and when there is an opening in the conversation, introduce yourself.
- Do not stay with one person for too long, even if you are enjoying his company: you are there to meet many people.

Disengage yourself by saying, "I do not want to take up too much of your time. I enjoyed talking with you."
■ Never stay until the end unless you are running the event. Leave when the crowd starts thinning out.
■ Always wear comfortable shoes and do not sit down unless everyone is sitting. Networking events are a great time to wear a bright jacket or scarf so that people can find you in the crowd.

There are many more informal ways to network on a one-on-one basis that can be just as or more effective in developing relationships than a planned event. Approach any party as a potential networking event.

■ "Stay in touch with friends and what they are doing."
■ "Network with people in other parts of your organization."
■ "Weddings are a great time to network with older professionals who can give you general career advice. Always remember to stick some business cards in your pocket or purse."

A significant minority of the women I spoke with insisted that I cover golf. Many of them had found golf to be a rare opportunity to spend four to five hours with a client or boss in a relaxed atmosphere. If you are in any type of sales function, golf can be a great career booster. Do not be intimidated if you do not already play. Use company events to join a golf clinic. Take some lessons at your local public course. Go to the driving range after work. A golf professional told me it takes abut three years to get comfortable on the course, which is a short time when considered in the context of a career. She also said that men often hit longer drives, but many women are better than men when putting and chipping. You may never be a great golfer, but you can still have a lot of fun.

■ "I learned to play golf with 20 women, and it has helped me in my career."
■ "You don't need to be a great player. Just have the right attitude, know the rules of etiquette, and play quickly so you do not hold up better players."

- "If you are concerned your play could hinder others, ask to be paired with people who are beginners."
- "I bought some low-end clubs, some golf shoes, and a couple of outfits, so I look the part even though I am still learning."

✓ **Takeaways:** Carve time out of your life for regular networking. Find several groups with which you share an interest and will enjoy spending your time. Learn to play golf since it is a great way to spend time with clients or colleagues.

Mentors

Most people had had mentors and found them extremely useful. What exactly is a mentor? One person provided a good definition:

- "A mentor is someone who helps you see outside yourself— what you need to learn to get ahead. A coach is someone who specifically tells you how to do something better."

What should you be looking for in a mentor? It can differ depending on what you need to learn to advance your career.

- "Mentoring is not usually a long-term situation. Does the person have skills that can help you now?"
- "I had to be proactive in finding mentors. I was looking for people who were successful and had a larger view of the world than I did."
- "I think a good mentor is someone three to five years further than you. Can you imagine being in that person's position? Do you want to be like him or her?"
- "I identified people who impressed me on different dimensions and I thought would have an interest in helping me."
- "It is important to be mentored by both men and women, since they have different perspectives."

People found mentors in different places. They were not always senior people and were often outside the company. Remember, a mentor helps you learn things, and that knowledge can come from various sources.

- "My first mentor was someone I supervised who was old enough to be my father. However, he taught me a lot about the business that I needed to know."
- "One of my mentors was my mother. She did not go to work until she raised her children, but she has an uncanny ability to assess people situations."
- "My greatest mentor was someone who worked for me. We mentored each other."
- "People who have left your company can be good mentors, since they know the organization and its culture."
- "Professional societies can be great places to find mentors."
- "I have a personal advisory committee. It is a mental list of people outside my organization that I talk to about career advice."

Mentors are not always easy to recruit. How do you form a relationship with a mentor? There are many ways.

- "Start out with a mentor on a casual basis. Just ask if you can have breakfast or lunch."
- "Never ask, 'Will you be my mentor?' It's like asking, 'Will you be my Valentine?'"
- "Approach someone in a less formal way. Say, 'May I ask you for career advice from time to time?'"
- "I stumbled into my two major mentors: a capable, credible individual in my firm who took me along as he rose up, and a client with whom I developed a deep and profitable relationship."

Formal mentoring programs exist at a number of companies, but they do not have a lot of support.

- "I was at a firm that assigned mentors, and it never worked. It was like a shotgun marriage."

- "When it's a formal program, people look at it as an obligation."
- "I am not a big fan of formal mentoring programs where women mentor women. It is too visible and it makes people nervous."

You will be judged on how well you use the mentor's time, so come prepared and discuss subjects where the mentor can add value.

- "The person being mentored should take the responsibility to schedule the meeting and come prepared with questions or send them in advance. Anything discussed should not go beyond the two people, unless it is agreed the mentor will take some action."
- "Use your mentor for strategic counseling on what to work on next, political advice, what skills you need to improve, how you can be heard, and as a sounding board on different paths you can take."
- "As a mentor, I prefer when people present me with alternatives and ask me to weigh in."
- "I can't do all the work for them. They need to come in prepared."
- "A mentor is only a sounding board, so the mentee needs to make the sounds."
- "I tried to be as open with my mentors as I could. I trusted their judgment and good faith, and they helped guide me through events. It was easy for them to think which opportunities would motivate me, since I had been honest with them."

Several people made the distinction that very few mentors are willing to go out on a limb to help someone else. While you may be lucky enough to have a strongly supportive mentor, you should not expect this. Sometimes the relationship works, and sometimes it doesn't.

- "I break mentors into three categories: sponsors, coaches, and mentors. Sponsors are people who have political capital and are willing to use it to help you. These people will jump in early when you really need support. Coaches know the game and can give good advice but don't have much clout or are not willing to use it. Mentors usually don't do much, and at least half of them give bad advice."

- "You want a network of people who will pound the table when you are up for promotion, so factor that in and look for opportunities to work for people who genuinely like and respect you."
- "Don't expect the mentor to do anything other than give you advice."

Should you look for mentors who are similar to you in gender or race? Some people have found that senior people often are more willing to help people who are like themselves in some way.

- "I spent the first third of my career helping myself. The second third was helping my team. Now I want to help younger women."
- "I was more than happy to talk to younger women, especially about the issues around having children and working."
- "You need mentors who will be great ambassadors for you. This is especially important for women of color."

What are the mistakes people have made with their mentors or seen others make?

- "When I was a junior consultant, there was only one woman CEO in my industry concentration, and when I wrote and asked to have breakfast with her, she readily agreed. She had lots of great advice and then I did the dumbest thing. I did not stay in touch with her. I missed a great opportunity to maintain that relationship."
- "One young woman was very demanding and asked for favors that made me uncomfortable. You need to invest in a relationship before you ask too much."

Some people enjoy being mentors and some do not, so be careful whom you ask. See if you can find out if the person has mentored others.

- "Being a mentor is a rewarding experience if you take it seriously. I have taken kids out of college and helped them negotiate through departments, international assignments, and getting graduate degrees."
- "I have a gift of being able to see where people will grow to years before it will happen. I can see what is possible, how they should move around, and basic requirements they need."
- "I never like to mentor someone who works for me. I think it's a conflict."

What type of people did this group of senior executives *not* want to mentor? The list is longer than you might think. If you want to have a good relationship with mentors, make sure you do not exhibit any of these behaviors.

- "Mentoring is an implicit commitment, so I want to be sure someone has the capacity and potential to benefit from mentoring. Do they care about what I say, or are they just using me? Are they willing to listen?"
- "I do not want to waste my time on someone who is clueless. It may not be fair, but you can't help someone if the raw material is not there."
- "I would not mentor someone without integrity."
- "I will not mentor someone who is networking for networking's sake."
- "If someone is passive and not proactive, I don't feel I can help them."
- "I will not mentor someone who is emotionally needy. If you need constant affirmation, I'm not the one to fix you."
- "I don't like unhappy people or someone with a victim mentality. I don't want someone to use this relationship to complain."

✓ **Takeaways:** Mentors can provide an excellent sounding board and give objective career advice. Be proactive, schedule meetings, and come prepared with questions.

■ **Career-Enhancing Moves**

1. Develop networks inside and outside your company of people with whom you share common interests.
2. Find mentors who can provide perspective on your career. Be proactive in setting up meetings, and come prepared with discussion topics.
3. Train yourself to be a leader by assuming responsibility and projecting confidence in yourself and your work.
4. Use task forces as a way to gain skills and meet people, but be sure your primary work does not suffer.
5. Learn to play golf. Golf provides an easy opportunity to spend hours with someone you would like to know better.
6. Learn how to disengage from people at events when you have spent sufficient time with them.

■ **Career-Limiting Moves**

1. Do not waste your time networking with people you do not want to know.
2. Do not waste a mentor's time or ask your mentor to do something for you that she or he is not prepared to do.
3. Do not assume you cannot be a leader. Leaders come in many styles and you can find leadership opportunities that fit your personality.

Six

Dating, Emotions, and Office Politics: Watch for the Quicksand

In the workplace you are confronted with the issues of dating, fending off unwanted attention, expressing emotion, along with gossip and office politics. This chapter is definitely not from the employee handbook.

Dating at Work Is Dangerous Territory

If you are single when you start at a company, chances are you will date people you meet at work. No one seems to think dating at work is optimal, but several of the senior women met their husbands at work, and many more dated people at work. Knowing dating at work is far from ideal, how can people be as professional as possible?

Peer-to-peer dating is commonplace and the most acceptable form of dating, but it still has its problems. The important thing is to keep the relationship out of the office as much as possible. Some people recommend not letting anyone know about the relationship, but your company may have policies that your supervisor must be informed.

- "When you are new to a city and working all the time, where else are you going to meet people? It's OK if there is no reporting relationship, but it is better if you are not side by side every day."
- "Don't let the relationship be obvious or you will make others uncomfortable."
- "Two senior people at work have a relationship and you would never know. They are very good at compartmentalizing."

- "It only works well when it is very discreet and people do not know."
- "Peer-to-peer dating is OK in a large office as long as they let their supervisors know and do not work together. In small offices, it is a challenge."

The key concern of people at work appears to be the conversations that go on at home after work. Also, people always assume there is favoritism or teaming up, which is compounded when someone gets promoted.

- "There is always the question of whether the people dating are colluding on the side. The burden is on them to show an office relationship will work."
- "I dated a peer who was a longtime friend, but immediately people's attitudes changed toward me. They said they could not trust me with anything, since they knew it would get back to him. He then became my boss, which was even more of a problem and made it difficult for him to assign projects. We broke up, but the issue of people not trusting me persisted."
- "I have two people on my team dating, and it is very difficult. It throws off the open dialogue you are trying to create in an environment. They won't comment on each other's performance, and that's a problem."
- "When you put men and women together, you are going to have relationships, but someone ends up moving and it is usually the woman."
- "Sometimes people start dating, one of them gets promoted, and it's a struggle to figure out what to do."
- "You never know who will end up reporting to whom."

When you first start dating it all seems great, but when people break up and are in the same environment, there can be tension.

- "Peers dating peers is less of a problem, especially when people are young, but when they break up it's a problem."

- "When people break up, it is very awkward. One or both of them end up leaving the department."
- "People get very emotional, especially when the relationship does not work out. They lose all perspective."

Even bigger issues arise when one of the people is in a senior position. It often does not turn out well, and it is usually the subordinate who suffers.

- "When a woman starts to date a senior person, it puts her in a compromising position. People start to question her every move."
- "Dating someone you work for is absolutely a no-no."
- "At our firm we had a partner dating an associate. Even though management spoke to both about keeping the personal and professional issues separate and they were not staffed on the same deals, it was a problem."
- "When a woman starts dating a senior person, the problem is her peers. They think she is getting better assignments and is not being reviewed honestly."

Occasionally you end up dating someone who can be physically threatening, and the fact that you work together makes it difficult to get legal help.

- "I dated a senior person and learned the hard way what a problem it was. When I broke it off he turned into a stalker, and even though he broke into my apartment I could not get a restraining order, since we worked together."

People agree dating clients is very dangerous both for you and your firm.

- "Don't date a client. It's like walking a plank."
- "Dating a client undermines the credibility of your firm."
- "If you start dating a client, talk with a senior person and get reassigned."
- "I had a young woman come in and confess she had fallen

in love with a client and was ready to resign. It turned out her partner was confessing to his boss the same day. The senior client person and I talked, and we ended up just reassigning both of them. They are now happily married, but that does not always happen."

The one absolute taboo is dating someone who is married. No matter how people feel about the spouse, they will not approve. Love does not conquer all.

- "If you are involved with a married man, that is an affair, not a relationship."
- "I was at a firm where many of the senior partners were fooling around with younger women. The men thought they were masters of the universe and the rules did not apply to them. The young women involved did not realize they were one in a long line of distractions. Many believed this was love and the men would actually leave their wife and children. Guess what? It never happened and the women all left the firm."
- "Young women need to open their eyes and realize they are just not that special to the guy."
- "I know one woman from work who left her husband and kids to be with a guy, and he still has not gotten a divorce."
- "When women get involved in an affair they make much more of a sacrifice than the man. While both parties' reputations are damaged, people say a man is having a midlife crisis, but the woman's reputation is permanently damaged."
- "The young woman usually gets shuttled off to some undesirable location."
- "I would fire anyone who is having an extramarital affair."
- "A woman in our firm got involved with a married man, and it was a career-ending event for both of them. Their assistants talked about it, everyone knew, and it showed poor judgment."

✔ **Takeaways:** Dating peers is acceptable, but you must be discreet. Dating a single senior person is dangerous, and you will feel resentment from peers. Having an affair with someone who is married is career suicide, and you risk losing your job.

If a Boss or Client Hits on You, Take Action

One of the most uncomfortable experiences in business is when a senior person hits on you and you are not interested. This can take several forms, and how you should react depends on your personality and the intent of the approach.

Women often look back and realize they were naive and got themselves into situations that could have been avoided if they had been a little more savvy. So what should you do? Try to remove yourself from the situation.

- "Your antennae need to be out at all times. If you think a client is interested, don't spend any time alone. He won't be able to ask you out in the middle of a conference room."
- "When you are in your 20s and 30s, you need to be suspicious of people who spend a lot of unproductive time with you. Don't set yourself up for a real pass, since that can be embarrassing."
- "When someone makes an advance, I ask myself what was there about my demeanor that suggested I was available and I try to change it."

Some people just put out feelers to see if the other party is interested. The easiest way to handle this is to make it clear that you are not interested.

- "Address it right then and there."
- "A polite 'No, thank you' is the easiest response."
- "One man kept asking me to meet for a drink to talk about

'work.' I told him I'd be happy to have a meeting in the office or breakfast, but I did not do drinks."
- "Just tell the person you are not comfortable going out."

Many people prefer the polite approach to handling a difficult situation and found that this worked for them.

- "I always try to give the person a gracious out. For example, I once said: 'I am terribly sorry if I inadvertently gave you the impression I was interested in something. I am not interested.'"
- "I try to use humor. When a client suggested he come up to my hotel room after dinner, I laughed and said sarcastically, 'Right. We'd really think that was a good idea when we woke up tomorrow.'"

Sometimes you just have to be a little more blunt to be sure the other person understands your lack of interest.

- "I told him, 'If that was a pass, I don't appreciate it, and don't do it again.'"
- "A potential client said to me, 'Next time we meet, why don't we meet at your apartment?' I looked him in the eye and said, 'Our successful meeting was based on my intellect, nothing more.'"

Everyone says that if you handle a low-key situation and it never happens again, just ignore it. You do not need to embarrass the person by ever bringing it up again. If there is unwanted physical contact or sexual harassment, you need to be more aggressive in your own defense.

- "If there is physical contact, talk to someone in your organization if you are not comfortable dealing with the situation yourself."
- "Most people just complain to a peer, and that does not help. If it is serious, you need to go higher up."
- "I had a boss try to force himself into my hotel room. I went to another member of management and complained.

I changed departments, but that was OK with me because I did not want to report to him. It turned out well since people felt I had been serious and professional in how I handled the situation."

Do not overreact to a situation. Some people are politically incorrect, and while you may be able to force your company to reprimand them, you are not going to change them. If they are not interfering with your performance, consider whether you need to escalate the issue.

- "Some older men treat young women like daughters. Remember to choose your battles. If it is intentional, say something. If it is benign, ignore it."
- "Don't be a drama queen."
- "Don't overreact if someone gives you a real compliment."

While the women had useful advice, much of it was in hindsight and they admitted they did not react well at the time they were approached.

- "I had a boss who would call my hotel room, knock on my door, and had a wandering hand when dancing at company events. As a young woman I felt I had to handle it on my own, so I just ignored him."
- "There was a senior married man who told me, 'I find you very attractive.' At a company party he invited me to slow dance, and his hands were all over me until a friend's husband rescued me. I did not know what to do and found a way to transfer out of the department. I later found out that he was doing the same thing to other women. I wish now I had reported him."

There is one thing everyone agrees on: do not get forced into anything.

- "Don't do anything you do not want to do. There will always be another job."

✔ **Takeaways:** You need to learn to deal with unwanted attention from senior people. If they are just testing the waters, politely but firmly make it clear you are not interested. If they get physically aggressive, report the incident to your company. Never do anything you do not want to do.

Save the Tears for the Movies

We all have emotions, but strong emotions make many people uncomfortable, particularly in the workplace. Companies differ, but the consensus was that many people are too emotional at work.

- "We are all real people with emotions, but people who are overly emotional do not do well in business."
- "Know your audience. You can share emotions with some people and not others."
- "Try to hold your emotions in check and present a balanced point of view."
- "Emotions are hard to control. That's why they are called emotions."

Emotion is an area where people perceive there are gender disparities. Whether or not this is true for you personally, you should recognize that many people believe the stereotypes for male and female emotional differences.

- "People get passionate about what they see as a wrong decision. For women a common reaction is to cry. Men are more likely to explode in anger."
- "We are just wired differently."
- "One male manager said he no longer wanted to work with a young woman because she was 'constantly taking her emotional temperature,' and he found it uncomfortable to work with her."
- "Men are suspect of women who are too emotional."

Every woman I asked said she had cried at work at one time or another, even if only in the bathroom, and several teared up just talking about the experience. However, everyone except one person felt it was not accepted in the business world and women must fight against an emotional reaction that includes tears.

- "Sometimes I feel my eyes filling up, and I know it is perceived as a weakness on my part."
- "You can say you are not going to break down, but for some of us, it's in our DNA."
- "We have a woman here who wells up constantly. It is tough on everybody."
- "Women get more penalized for their form of emotion (tears) than men (anger). Tears are not respected or appreciated. Tears may be more real than anger, but they are not accepted."
- "The workplace is more accommodating of someone blowing up than crying."
- "What I tell young women about crying is, 'It is better to be homicidal than suicidal.'"

The lone dissenter felt that crying was a natural emotion, and she had finally ended up at a place where it was accepted.

- "I should write a book called *I Cried My Way to the Top*. I only cried when I felt comfortable crying, and it is not unusual here. Many people, both men and women, have come into my office to cry. I never felt I had to do it the way a man did it. I worked in an environment before where crying did not work, but here it is fine."

There are very rare exceptions to the "no crying" rule.

- "We had an employee death, and both men and women were crying."
- "Someone heard at work that his son had cancer, and we all cried with him."

OK, so many women get emotional. What are some ways women have learned to handle this in the work environment?

- "If something happens and you start to get tears in your eyes, say, 'I did not expect this. Give me a minute.' Then regain your composure and go on with the conversation."
- "Now that I am older, I prepare more for bad news. I do more scenario planning in advance of meetings and manage my expectations better. When I am mentally prepared for a bad outcome, it does not surprise me and I am not emotional when it happens."
- "Take deep breaths. Maintain some semblance of control over the rest of the conversation."
- "If I start to tear up, I buy time by saying, 'Can you give me further clarification?'"
- "If you think you might cry, sit with your back to the door so that only the person you are talking to you knows you are crying."

All else fails and you are really crying. What now? Women had very different advice that ranged from leaving the meeting to using the other person's discomfort to get what you want.

- "If you are crying and you do not know what you want to do, get out of the situation."
- "If I am stuck in a situation that is so emotional I cannot handle it, I defer the conversation until I can get my emotions in check."
- "I left a meeting and went for a walk around the parking lot."
- "Don't use tears as a reason to disengage. If the reason you are upset is disappointing news, you still need to address the issue and sometimes it is hard to get the conversation back."
- "Crying can be to your advantage if the person on the other side of the table is taken aback by your reaction. He would rather not have you upset, so maybe you can negotiate something you could not get at another time."

People disagree about whether anger is an acceptable emotion at work, so this may be an area where the culture of the company comes into play concerning what is normal and acceptable. For some people, anger is deliberate and calculated.

- "Anger is viewed as a negotiating technique to be used in some situations. It is a way of making your point."
- "I have stormed out of a room as a deliberate negotiation move, but in the office I am fairly calm."
- "If you are going to use anger strategically, it needs to be controlled anger. You need to sound powerful, not panicky, so watch the pitch of your voice and choose your words carefully."
- "Anger is OK if used judiciously. Someone who uses anger is perceived as having authority."
- "Many successful businessmen have gotten things done by table pounding."

Often anger does not go over well, especially when used by women. You need to know your audience before you decide whether it is a useful tool for a particular situation.

- "I really dislike anger. I fired a man who worked for me because he was too volatile."
- "Law school teaches you how to argue about everything, but I found in business that an aggressive style can be off-putting to many people."
- "I had a guy start screaming on a conference call because he lost a deal point. I told him to call back when be could be more professional and hung up. He called right back and acted like nothing happened."
- "Sometimes a woman gets more attention when she raises her voice. The problem is, it is a fine line between being assertive, which is good, and being aggressive, which is not."
- "When a woman shows anger or aggressiveness, she runs the risk of being tagged as a bitch."
- "If you are angry you should make a statement such as 'I

am angry with what you have said' to make it clear it is not personal."

Anger, like crying, is not always easily controlled, and you may not always achieve the desired result.

- "If I could be angry without being upset I would, but I can't."
- "When I get angry, I lose control and can say things I can't take back."

Anger works two ways. You may find yourself on the receiving end of someone else's anger. You can ask the person to change his style when working with you, or if you are not comfortable doing that, get another opinion on how to handle the situation. Unfortunately, if you are in a company where this type of behavior is tolerated, you will have to learn to deal with the person or change jobs.

- "If you are working for someone with a bullying style, tell the person, 'This is not working for me.'"
- "Talk to someone who knows the person to get advice on what to do."

People like working with positive colleagues, but choose your subjects carefully and watch your level of enthusiasm.

- "It is good to be passionate on an idea and champion it, but use passion selectively. If you are passionate about everything, then people will think you are not really passionate about anything."
- "When we win some business around here, we all get excited."
- "It is great to have enthusiasm and be upbeat."
- "If someone is excited all the time, they can come across as juvenile or 'lacking gravitas.'"
- "We have a woman at work who is so enthusiastic about the local sports team that it borders on obsession. It makes people think she is strange."
- "Sad is never good."

Humor can be useful in a business situation, but as with enthusiasm, choose your subjects with caution.

- "In a service business, you better learn to lose with humor, since in most games you do not have a .300 batting average."
- "When I lose a piece of business from a client, I say something like, 'Always the bridesmaid, but remember next time I already have the dress in the closet.'"
- "Women need to be careful how they joke with men. Jokes cannot be off-color and certainly not relate to them personally."

✔ **Takeaways:** Watch all your emotions at work. Crying is not good, since it is perceived as a weakness and undermines your professionalism. Anger, if used to make a point, can be acceptable, but must be very controlled. Enthusiasm about the company and business is always positive.

Avoid Gossip

Whether it is the latest news about a pending reorganization or a rumor that someone is pregnant, everyone agrees that spreading gossip is not a good thing. You may call it office politics, but it is just gossip by another name. The worst thing about engaging in this behavior is that it can make people lose trust in you and cut you out of the loop.

- "When I hear someone repeat things that they were obviously asked to keep confidential, it lowers my respect for that person."
- "Many companies are on a 'need to know' basis and if you gossip, people will not trust you."
- "As a boss, I am furious when I hear people repeating incorrect information. It is impossible not to affect how I feel about the person who is spreading the rumors."

If you must talk about the latest office rumors, be very careful in whom you confide.

- "You had better know the people you are talking to and that they will put the information in the right context."
- "Never gossip with a boss."
- "You need to be conscious of what is going on around you, but you can listen without repeating things."
- "A peer might use the gossip as a way to undermine your credibility."

You must also think about the time you are wasting by gossiping, since others do.

- "Be careful how much time you spend chatting with people. It can be very time-consuming."
- "If someone is gossiping, it tells me she does not have enough to do."

Would you want personal things you thought you had told someone in confidence repeated? How would you feel if someone you did not know heard the information?

- "Before you share information about another person, ask yourself how that person would feel if he or she knew you were telling someone."
- "Coming up in the elevator I just heard a young woman telling some colleagues (as well as strangers like me) that a coworker's unmarried teenage sister is pregnant. I wanted to kill her, and it wasn't even my sister!"

Many people admitted they had gossiped when they knew they should not have, but it is tantalizing to be perceived as an insider.

- "Occasionally I pass something on, and as soon as it is out of my mouth I ask myself, 'Now, why did I say that?'"
- "I never initiate gossip, but if someone drops in and starts speculating on something that may happen at the company, I don't act like a jerk and leave."
- "In our company, rumors spread like wildfire: promotions, firings, new assignments. I know I should not get involved

in these conversations, but I'm worried that if I don't ever say anything, people think I am not in the loop."

✔ Takeaways: Do not gossip, regardless of the subject. It is much better for your career that you be viewed as discreet and as someone who can be trusted with confidential information.

▪ Career-Enhancing Moves

1. Control your emotions at work. This will reinforce your reputation as a professional.
2. Do not engage in gossip or office politics if you want to be viewed as someone who can be trusted with confidential information.
3. If you must date at work, be very discreet and stay at the peer level in a different department.
4. Learn to avoid or gracefully turn away unwanted advances.

▪ Career-Limiting Moves

1. Do not cry at work. It is unprofessional and will make people take you less seriously.
2. Do not violate a confidence.
3. Do not have an affair with someone who is married.

Seven

What to Wear: Style Influences Success

When you walk into a room, people have formed an opinion of you based on your appearance before you even open your mouth to say hello. Many people feel that women are judged more harshly than men on their appearance. This may result from the lack of a standard "uniform" for women, regardless of whether the dress code is traditional business or business casual. The variation in women's attire can be either an advantage or a disadvantage. Lack of attention to appearance can lead to a negative impression, whereas a creative but professional outfit can allow a woman to stand out and be noticed in a positive way.

- "Dress in an elegant way. Not sexy, but not blue suit either. Then when you open your mouth and say something smart, people will be blown away."
- "There is a lot of power in your clothes. Find your own style."
- "Dress stylishly but conservatively."
- "You want to look pulled together, professional, strong."
- "Clothes make the woman."

For all clothing, the word I heard most often was "quality," followed closely by "professional."

- "It is not about the variety of your wardrobe. It is about the quality."
- "Make the investment to buy expensive clothes. Most everything will need to be dry-cleaned."
- "Don't wear anything that distracts or suggests other than a professional demeanor."
- "If you feel the least bit uncomfortable when you look in the mirror, don't wear it."

Poor dress can have an impact on your career, and some companies and people will judge you more harshly than others.

- "If someone has no flair in her appearance, I think of it as the equivalent of not speaking up. It tells me a lot about the person's self-esteem."
- "Minor errors accumulate and can impact your career, so consider your appearance carefully."
- "The wrong wardrobe gives people misimpressions of your abilities."
- "Don't be too conservative or boring. You want people to remember you."

Notice how senior women in your organization dress and emulate that style. In some companies, there is more leeway than others.

- "Look at the leaders in your company and dress they way they do."
- "In New York everyone wears black, but in the rest of the country they wear more color. Color does not necessarily mean more feminine, just less traditional business attire."
- "There is a lot more bandwidth to express yourself in the media and entertainment world than in other industries."

You send a message by what you are wearing, so make sure you consciously decide what message you want to send, particularly for special events or meetings. Also remember that you can be pulled into a meeting with senior people or clients unexpectedly.

- "I always wear a suit when I meet with clients. I don't want to have a click down in their eyes if they think I am not dressed well."
- "Think about your audience. Some days you can wear clothes that are inappropriate on other days."
- "If you are wearing too much money, it sends a signal to clients that they are paying too much."

The other two basic pieces of advice were about style and knowing yourself.

- "Ask yourself what looks good on your body."
- "Be yourself. Wear what makes you feel good."

Very few women are blessed with a perfect body or fit exactly into the standard sizes, so find a good dressmaker and have your clothes tailored to your figure.

✔ **Takeaways:** Show confidence in yourself through your appearance. Dress stylishly but conservatively. Buy quality clothes. Get a good tailor and use her.

The Main Attraction: Business Attire Means a Suit

Traditional business attire means the equivalent of a suit. Pant suits are just as acceptable as a suit with a skirt and in many cases preferable, since pants allow more freedom of motion. When you are wearing pants you do not have to worry about a skirt riding up when you sit down in a meeting or how much skin you are showing when you cross your legs. The skirt and jacket can be different colors and fabrics as long as they were intended to be worn as an outfit and it meets the quality standards of a suit.

Women have a great deal of flexibility in the type of suit they wear, and different women have adopted different styles to fit their own personalities and companies.

- "I always wear a suit, and I like them with skirts."
- "You don't always have to wear a black pants suit."
- "Make sure the suit does not look like a school uniform on you. It should be more stylish."
- "How much you travel will determine what you buy. Silks and cottons don't travel well."
- "You will find one or two designers whose clothes look good on you."
- "Skirts should never be above the knee."

Many women feel you should start out on the conservative side when you join a company. You should also be cautious when dealing with clients who may have different standards from those of your own company.

- "At the beginning of your career, play on the conservative side."
- "You want to be accepted for who you are, but what image do you want to project?"
- "The younger you are, the less room you have to deviate from whatever is considered professional in your company."
- "Your attire is a message to the rest of the group how you consider yourself."
- "I always dress up for all meetings outside the office."

✔ **Takeaways:** Suits are the gold standard of professionalism, but they do not have to be boring to be powerful. Pants suits are just as acceptable as suits with skirts.

Business Casual Is a Minefield for Women

When most people think of business casual for a man, they think of khakis and a polo shirt. Ask 10 people to describe business casual for a woman, and it is unlikely two people would give the exact same answer.

Business casual is the most dangerous type of dress for women since it only takes one person in authority to decide you look unprofessional to impact your career. The first thing to remember is that business casual is not what you wear on the weekend: it is an entirely separate wardrobe. If you change from a company with a business dress code to one with a business casual dress code, you need to go out and buy new work clothes.

- "Some people mistakenly blend their work and personal lives, and their wardrobes reflect that. I have a serious work wardrobe."

Business casual is not easily defined, but the word to remember is "business." Pants and blouses should not be too tight. Watch how many buttons you leave undone.

- "Business clothes need to be more expensive, made of good fabrics, and be well tailored. The outfit should look pulled together."
- "Women's version of business casual is not khakis, even if the men are wearing them. You should wear tailored pants. Think the bottom part of a suit."
- "You should always have a jacket or jacket-like look such as a sweater set, and always be sure to put it on if you are going to a meeting."
- "Some young women here look like they are about to go to class. Their clothes are rumpled, young, unserious."
- "Young women think business casual is what they wore at college, and it's not. In college you dress for show. Here the objective is not to have people focus on the fact that you are attractive but to focus on your work."
- "I always wear a jacket. It just feels better."

I heard a lot of "not," "no," and "never" when people tried to describe business casual.

- "Not too sexy. Not too funky."
- "Not too short, too tight, or too suggestive. This is not the type of attention you want."
- "Not too much skin."
- "No sundresses. No strappy shirts."
- "No tank tops with built-in bras."
- "No stretch pants."
- "Never look like you are going to the beach or the gym."
- "If it is appropriate for a nightclub or the beach, it is not appropriate for work."
- "Sporty casual, such as tank tops, is too much like Saturday attire."

A number of people mentioned that it is better to err on the side of dressing up than dressing down, especially when you are new in a company.

- "Dress for the company culture, but dress up to the job you want to have."
- "It is hard to be taken seriously or be viewed as a leader when you dress like a 22-year-old."
- "In the business world it is always better to be overdressed. It suggests that you care and are trying harder."
- "If your outfit is ever distracting, it dilutes your ability to be effective."
- "Some of my peers have criticized me for dressing too formally, but my boss told me to keep dressing the way I do. He prefers it to the way the others are dressed."

While some companies allow jeans on Fridays, nearly all of our senior women thought wearing jeans was a bad idea.

- "Differentiate yourself. When others are wearing jeans on Fridays, dress one notch better than your peers."
- "I have a problem with people who look like they are dressed to weed the garden."

If you are pregnant, remember one thing about maternity clothes: you need to look professional at a time when you may not always feel your best. You will be wearing these clothes for many months, so consider them an investment and buy a few high-quality maternity outfits. If you have seen professional maternity clothes on a friend, ask if you can borrow them, since many women will gladly lend them. Don't even consider the belly-hugging fashions popular among celebrities. Also, stay with your style. If you always wear dark suits, this is not the time to experiment with a flowered print dress. People notice what you are wearing during these months, and you do not want to give off unintended signals by lack of attention to your appearance.

- "I remember one partner who had outgrown all of her clothes toward the end of her pregnancy and started wearing farm overalls to work. I thought she could have done better."

✔ **Takeaways:** Business casual is not the same as your weekend attire but is an entirely separate wardrobe. Clothes should be tailored, serious, and look like an outfit. If you are pregnant, wear professional maternity clothes.

Tops Should Focus on Coverage, Not Cleavage

Tops are a wonderful way to add color and style to any outfit. Many women use a brightly colored silk blouse to soften a conservative suit.

- "I always wear a silk blouse with a suit."
- "I love bright colors and look everywhere I go for great blouses that can be worn under a suit."

Always remember these three rules:

- No cleavage.
- Not too tight.
- No bare midriff.

How do you tell where to draw the line? Think of how you are seen by others—not just when you are standing in front of a mirror, but in an active work environment where you move around.

- "If someone can see down your blouse when you bend down, it is cut too low."
- "Close-fitting clothes are fine, but ask yourself if a male colleague would be uncomfortable."
- "Don't accentuate your breasts. Your top should not be too sheer, and someone should never be able to see your nipples."

Others had more specific suggestions for tops.

- "Sleeveless tops are too casual for work."
- "No halter tops."

✔ **Takeaway:** Tops should never be too tight, too low cut, or too sheer.

Shoes Can Be Your Guerrilla Fashion Item

Shoes are one area in which women often rebel against a traditional business dress code, and many admitted that their shoes were the most fashionable part of their wardrobe.

- "I love the way shoes can add color or detail to an otherwise boring suit. It's also great knowing they will always fit—even if I have not been to the gym lately."
- "Shoes can be sexier."
- "You must have beautiful shoes. Quality matters here."
- "Don't wear big clunky earth shoes. You'll look too much like a college student."
- "Boots are great, especially with business casual."

Be careful of one thing: your shoes need to be well maintained. Many men are very conscious of keeping their own shoes polished and some will equate scuffed, unpolished shoes or rundown heels with sloppy work.

- "Even if you are short on money, always keep your shoes polished and your heels in good shape."

There were a few other good tips.

- "Buy comfortable shoes. You spend a lot of time at work."
- "Make sure your shoes do not make a lot of noise when you walk."

Open-toed shoes and sandals got mixed reactions, mostly because it was felt women did not always wear them well.

- "Women wear sandals at times that are inappropriate. They can have a great outfit and then ruin it with sandals that are too casual."
- "Open-toed shoes are OK, but if you are wearing stockings be sure there is no reinforced toe."
- "If you wear sandals or open-toed shoes, you need to have a fresh pedicure."

Whether the dress code specifies it or not, our women recommend that two types of footwear stay out of the office: sneakers and flip-flops. The only exception was sneakers for the walk-to-work crowd in a city, and even there people felt you should change to work shoes as soon as you got to your desk.

✔ **Takeaways:** Shoes can be very fashionable and add style to traditional business dress. They should always be polished and well maintained.

Dress Up an Outfit with Jewelry and Scarves

One criticism heard of young women was that they often did not "complete" an outfit. A scarf or some jewelry can make an outfit looked more finished and the wearer appear more sophisticated. You just need to be sure the jewelry is appropriate for your outfit.

Jewelry is a hot topic among women. This is another area in which women can express individuality, and every woman I met was wearing some jewelry. How much and what type depends on the company and geographic location.

- "Pearl earrings, small gold or silver earrings or hoops, and diamond studs are always OK. Just stay away from large, expensive pieces."
- "Wear something tailored but not too big."
- "You want your jewelry to make you look 'stylish' and not like a 'kept woman.'"
- "If you earned it yourself, you can wear it."
- "Jewelry can make a real statement. Some women can wear large artsy jewelry and get away with it."
- "Some women wear ethnic pieces that are very powerful."
- "Jewelry can be an icebreaker. Whenever I wear my silver and turquoise necklace, someone asks me where I got it."
- "I collect jewelry when I travel, and it always brings back good memories. It makes a business suit less masculine."

- "Jewelry is a much better way to express yourself than a short skirt."

The only controversy around jewelry was diamonds, and this seemed to do mostly with company culture and geographic location. However, some people believed diamonds make a moral statement.

- "It is always OK to wear your engagement ring."
- "I would never wear diamond earrings to the office. I work with people who could never afford them, so I think it is inappropriate to wear them."
- "Once I testified at a mock jury trial, and they said they hated me because I was wearing diamond earrings."

Just be careful the jewelry is not distracting. A bracelet that bangs on the table every time you write is an example of something that is not appropriate for an office.

- "Don't wear long, dangling earrings."
- "A woman was wearing a pearl on a gold chain that came out of a turtleneck just below her chin. Even time she spoke the pearl bobbed up and down and went in various directions. I can't remember what she said, but I still remember how distracting the pearl necklace was."

✔ **Takeaways:** Jewelry can add personality and style to an outfit. Be careful about wearing expensive or distracting pieces, and consider the company environment.

The Key Word Is "Under"

Underwear is just that: something to be worn under. It sounds simple, but for some people it is not that easy.

- "I never want to see someone's underwear, and women should always wear a bra, even if they think they do not need one."

- "Bras should have some substance. If you get cold, you do not want your nipples to stick out."
- "Panty lines are awful."
- "If you are wearing a thong, make sure it is covered up."
- "Wear great underwear if you want, but no one else needs to see it."

Many women realized they use underwear to improve their appearance and suggested others should do the same.

- "Make an honest assessment of your body. If you are going to have a lot of jiggle, wear pantyhose or some other type of control."
- "A woman was wearing a great pants suit and had taken off her jacket when she got up to get lunch. When she turned around, it was clear she must have been wearing a thong and no stockings, since her rear end was moving in every direction."

The one area where people had different opinions was stockings: to wear or not to wear. This is another area where company culture comes into play.

- "I know many women have stopped wearing stockings, but bare legs look awful."
- "If you are not wearing stockings, you better have great looking, well-shaved legs."
- "If you are very tan, I guess it's OK."
- "I've often gone without stockings under pants, but this past summer was the first time I wore a good suit without stockings."
- "We think less highly of men who don't wear socks, so why should it be OK for women not to wear stockings?"

✓ Takeaways: Underwear for work is meant to cover up, not enhance, your feminine assets. It should never be visible.

Coats Are Not Just to Keep You Warm

The impression you make starts with your coat. While it sounds obvious, many people just grab whatever is in the hall closet and do not think about whether the coat complements the rest their outfit. If you are wearing a suit jacket or blazer, your coat should at least cover the jacket. The style should match the rest of the outfit, meaning that even a long ski jacket does not go well with a formal suit.

- "Don't show up to a business meeting in a parka."
- "You need more than one coat. Get a heavy one for winter and a lighter-weight one for spring and fall. Your spring coat can be used when it's raining if you do not have a good rain coat."

Coats last for years, so consider them investments and go for quality. Many people prefer to buy classic styles and add fashionable scarves, hats, or gloves if they are worried they will look too plain.

There was one huge geographic difference of opinion: fur coats. The New York City women I interviewed believed fur was always acceptable, whereas virtually all of the other women interviewed from other parts of the country only wore fur in social situations and many felt it was never acceptable for work.

- "If you are successful enough to have bought your own fur coat, then wear it, but if your daddy bought it for you, it will tick people off."
- "It is OK for a woman to send a message that she is very successful."

✔ **Takeaways:** A coat is a long-term investment, so you should buy for quality. Your coat should cover any suit jacket and be the same style as your outfit.

Purses and Briefcases

Your purse and briefcase are items that change less frequently than clothes and are seen often by many people, so quality is important.

- "Always have a great purse and briefcase."
- "It is more important to have one high-quality purse than nine purses of lower quality that match every outfit."

For briefcases, some people liked leather, others preferred the lighter weight of nylon. However, the briefcase needs to be practical. There were conflicting opinions on whether the utility of a backpack outweighed its youthful image.

- "The junior person will be carrying the material, so make sure you have at least one briefcase large enough to carry a lot of work."
- "If you show up with a backpack, people will think of you as a college kid."
- "We focus on safety at this company. Backpacks are much better for your back, so a lot of people here use them."

✔ **Takeaways:** Your purse is a major part of your wardrobe. Make sure it is high quality. A briefcase should be professional, large enough to carry extra work, and not a backpack.

Hair and Makeup

It is not enough to have a great wardrobe. You need to pay serious attention to how you personally look.

- "If you have not taken the time to be acceptably groomed, people will think you do not pay attention to details at work and you have a sloppy thought process."

Hair needs to have style, be appropriate for a work environment, and look good for your entire workday. Find a great hairdresser who takes night and weekend appointments.

- "A good haircut is critical. A simple style is best."
- "Long hair especially needs to be well cut and maintained."
- "Your hair style should not be so fussy that you have to attend to it several times a day."

- "Don't come into work with wet hair. Blow it dry before you come to work."

Everyone had certain styles they particularly disliked.

- "Some women just wrap their hair around and fasten it to the top of their heads with a clip, leaving the hair going in all directions. It looks ridiculous."
- "A ponytail makes you look very young."
- "Unruly curly hair looks very messy."
- "My pet peeve is hair hanging in someone's face."
- "In this company, big hair is not acceptable."

Makeup needs to be carefully applied. The extremes of too much makeup or no makeup are not recommended.

- "The younger generation errs on the side of too little makeup."
- "When you are young, wearing some makeup gives you power."
- "You need some amount of makeup to show you are serious."
- "If your makeup is appropriate for evening, it is not appropriate for the office. Especially watch the eye makeup."
- "When I was younger I was told I wore too much blush. I was trying for a little color, but I guess I went too far."

Several women mentioned perfume and nails as potential problem areas.

- "Too much perfume is a big issue."
- "One of my colleagues has a lot of allergies, so I had to give up perfume altogether."
- "A woman transferred from another part of the country and used a lot of perfume and had long red fingernails. All the women hated her. Someone finally took her aside and told her to tone it down."

There are several other items people felt needed to be mentioned that fall in the appearance category.

- "The only body part I want to see pierced is ears."
- "If you have an ankle tattoo, wear dark stockings."
- "There was an analyst who was chewing gum as we headed off to a client meeting. I told him he sounded like a cow and to get rid of it."

✔ **Takeaway:** A good haircut and judicious use of makeup are important to being seen as a professional.

Your Wardrobe Should Not Be Susceptible to Malfunction

Before you wear anything to the office, think of what could go wrong. In business, it is called scenario planning, so apply it to your clothes as well. There were some great stories about clothes that did not work well in business settings.

- "I was at lunch in a restaurant with a young coworker when an older woman came over and whispered in her ear. She turned bright red, and only later could I coax the conversation out of her. Apparently the woman said, 'Dear, could you please pull your top over the back of your pants? My husband can't take his eyes off the top of your thong.' The young woman never wore low-riding pants to work again without a jacket over them."
- "There was a woman who used to visit our company wearing beautiful suits. The problem was, once she sat down the tight skirts ended up just below her crotch. The guys never remembered what she said. All they talked about was whether anyone caught the color of her underwear."
- "I used to regularly stay at a hotel with a nice pool, and my male colleagues and I usually went swimming before dinner. One evening we joined a water polo game in progress and as I jumped up to hit the ball my bikini top came

undone and ended up around my waist. Ever since then I have traveled with a one-piece bathing suit designed for swimmers."

✔ Takeaway: Make sure your business clothes can handle active movement while remaining professional.

The Company Party Is Not the Place to Show Off

One of the most difficult decisions is what to wear to the holiday party or summer outing. This is not the place to roll out that great clingy dress or sheer sundress. Remember that it is business and you may be seeing senior people you do not know well. Add to your list of wardrobe necessities several nice but conservative outfits you can wear to these events.

- "I have a black silk pants suit I wear with different colored tops for office parties."
- "I wear a black dress with a bright jacket."
- "For the company outing I'd suggest khaki pants or a knee-length skirt, a nice top, and good sandals."

✔ Takeaway: Essential wardrobe items are nice but conservative dressy outfits and good casual clothes to be worn to company parties.

■ Career-Enhancing Moves

1. Develop a professional business appearance that fits your company's style.
2. Wear the highest-quality clothes you can afford.
3. Always have several traditional business suits in your closet, even if your company is business casual.

4. Dress on the dressy side of business casual.
5. Wear great shoes, and make sure they are always polished.
6. Find a good tailor and hairdresser, and use them often.

■ Career-Limiting Moves

1. Do not wear anything too tight, too short, too low cut, or too sheer.
2. Do not wear clothes that might make your colleagues uncomfortable.

Eight

Business Travel: It's All Business

Business and leisure travel are significantly different, so even if you have traveled widely on vacations, do not assume you know the rules of business travel. In business the objective is to make the trip as short as possible to get the work accomplished successfully. Business travelers have developed a travel routine but also learned to be flexible in dealing with the inevitable vagaries of life on the road. It is this ability both to move confidently through airports, hotels, and unfamiliar conference rooms, and to adapt to unplanned circumstances when necessary, that will make a businessperson a successful business traveler.

There is one other thing to remember: your colleagues, bosses, and clients are watching you while you travel and forming opinions of you.

- "Travel lets you see what fabric people are made of. How do they treat people? How resourceful are they when faced with the stresses of travel? Can they roll with the punches?"
- "When things go wrong, try to be resourceful in helping to solve the problems. Don't let your demeanor add stress to the situation."

What will make travel easier? There are some obvious and not so obvious suggestions.

If You Can't Carry It, Don't Bring It

Assume everyone you travel with will be carrying his or her luggage on board and that you need to do the same. Women generally can travel for four to seven days with a carry-on, although one woman claimed she could travel for three weeks with a small bag. What are the secrets to being well dressed with so few clothes? Advance planning.

- "I stay with one color theme, with two suits or pants suits, several blouses, a couple of scarves and simple jewelry. You can do a lot of mixing and matching."
- "Dark colors are best for travel. They do not show the wear."
- "The clothes need to pack well and not wrinkle. I use one of those suitcase inserts that keeps all the folded clothes together."
- "I never travel with expensive jewelry or fragile clothes. There is a lot of wear and tear on travel clothes, and items have occasionally disappeared from my hotel rooms."
- "I have clothes I know will get through security without setting off any alarms."
- "Remember anything in your carry-on may be prominently displayed at the security checkpoint if they open your bag. I was very sorry I packed some sexy red underwear when all my colleagues got a good look at it at security."

Packing for an international trip can be more complicated. If you are not sure what is normal, do some research ahead of time.

- "Think about the customs of the country where you are traveling. There are places where you can offend people with your attire."
- "You are a guest in someone else's country and culture. In many parts of the world you need a long-sleeved blouse and need to be as covered up as possible."
- "For U.S. multinationals, business casual has gone abroad. However, in major cities in Europe our managers still prefer formal business attire."
- "If you are unsure, dress conservatively."

Many women mentioned shoes as being a critical consideration for travel.

- "You need to be able to run to catch a plane. I can run in my high heels—and have."

- "Comfortable shoes are important. You will probably be doing a lot of walking."

Be prepared for short-notice business trips by having travel items in one spot. Do not assume you can buy anything where you are going since you will likely spend most of your time working.

- "I have a separate travel case for toiletries and cosmetics ready to go at all times."
- "I can pack for a week in five minutes. My travel items are all in one drawer, and I know what clothes travel well."
- "I carry a full complement of over-the-counter medicines for a cold, headaches, or upset stomach and have used them often."
- "I have a travel phone charger in my suitcase so that I do not forget it."

Always pack a little extra in case your trip is delayed or there are unforeseen circumstances.

- "I always have extra underwear."
- "I always bring a change of clothes in case something gets spilled on me."
- "Our meeting was planned for the city but got moved to a rural location. I was glad I had some pants and good walking shoes."
- "We had a deal that kept our team out of town longer than planned, and one young woman showed up the last day in orange hot pants. She ran out of clothes. We all still talk about it."

Your luggage is an extension of your wardrobe, and you will be judged by its practicality and appearance.

- "I travel with a rolling bag. It is easier on my back than one I have to carry and there is no strap to wrinkle my jacket."
- "A nice carry-on in nylon or leather is good, but never carry a gym bag."

- "You need to be able to carry it and lift it into an overhead compartment yourself."
- "People who travel light are looked at as successful. People who travel heavy are looked at as a joke."
- "We used to joke about a woman who looked like she was bringing a trunk with her."
- "One woman had an entire suitcase filled with shoes and purses to match every outfit."

There are times when checking luggage is appropriate such as a long trip or when bringing golf clubs to an outing. However, the key is to fit in with your fellow business travelers. If you are not sure if people will be checking, ask in advance.

- "Don't have more luggage than everyone else."
- "You never want to delay the others."

✔ **Takeaways:** Pack lightly and have a high-quality carry-on suitcase. Select clothes that travel well. Never check luggage except for very long trips.

When You Travel, You Are Your Company

While traveling on business, you represent your company to everyone you meet. The way you look and act will reflect on the firm.

The way you dress on the road is the most obvious opportunity for people to judge you.

- "Clothes for business travel are no different than what you would wear to a business meeting."
- "If you are traveling during the week, dress in your normal business attire. On a weekend you can dress in business casual."
- "Travel in clothes that can go straight into a meeting. Even if you plan to go to your hotel first, if your flight

is late you may be going directly from the airport to work."

- "En route, dress comfortably, but professionally. You get treated differently by the travel industry if you are dressed well."

Senior people will be watching you to see if you maintain your firm's image on the road, and some may have very high standards. If you are traveling with clients, follow their lead.

- "I was traveling with a team where one of our young colleagues was having stomach problems. She was drinking an over-the-counter remedy directly out of the bottle at the gate as we waited for our plane. Unfortunately, our CEO was on his way to another plane and saw this. He walked over to the woman and told her he was sorry she was not feeling well, but professionals at our firm did not guzzle medicine in public and she should go to the ladies room. She was mortified."
- "Don't upgrade, even with miles, if your client does not upgrade."

Much of your travel time will be spent in public places such as planes, airports, and restaurants. Most people know not to read a confidential presentation on a crowded plane, but one person had a story of how easy it is to forget about confidentiality when in a remote location.

- "After 10 days of traveling in Asia, my colleague and I went to a small restaurant where we were the only people speaking English. We were very tired and got into a discussion of the CEO and all his faults. Midway through our meal, the unassuming Japanese man sitting at the table next to ours got up and on his way out stopped by our table, gave us both his business card, and said, 'Say hello to your boss. He is a friend of mine.' Remember that the world is a village. Just because people are not speaking

English does not mean they do not understand everything you are saying."

✔ **Takeaways:** Represent your firm well while you travel. Dress and act professionally, and maintain confidentiality.

Off-Site Is Not Off-Duty

Many times the reason for the business trip is an off-site meeting at a resort location where sports are involved. It is important to remember that this is a business event and your clothes should be the equivalent of business attire.

- "No jeans, no short skirts, no flip-flops."
- "Golf shirts need to be pressed like a shirt. Don't look like your clothes just came out of the dryer."
- "If you are playing tennis, have a matching tennis outfit. If you are playing golf, wear long pants."
- "I ask myself, 'Do I want to be remembered in this outfit?'"
- "At our firm, off-site events are often held at clubs where partners are members. They consider every dress code infraction a personal insult."
- "Private clubs have rules, so be sure you know them."

Company or industry events are an excellent way to meet new people and make a good impression on senior people from your own firm. Remember that it is a business trip and do not get distracted by the new surroundings.

- "Even though it is team building, it is still an office event and I do not let my guard down."
- "Think about the image you want people to have of you. Many people may never have met you. What impression do you want to leave?"
- "This is a chance to make a good impression or not."
- "When the company is spending money to send you there, you are on the job 24/7."

✔ **Takeaways:** Off-site events are an extension of the office. Be sure your dress and your behavior reflect this.

Drinking Is Dangerous to Your Career

Traveling on business means dinner with colleagues, which may involve drinking before, during, and after dinner. Should you refrain from drinking? If not, how much is appropriate?

- "If you can drink some beer or wine and not have it affect you, OK, but don't ever get drunk."
- "Be very wary of dinners where the wine glasses keep getting filled. It is easy to lose track of how much you are drinking and say something stupid."
- "As people drink their behavior changes. If everyone is drinking, no one sees it, but the one person who isn't drinking notices it."
- "Trade shows have big parties, and many people drink too much."
- "Never drink the way you drink with your friends. You will never be sorry you did not drink too much."
- "You need to be aware that drinking and men and women traveling together are a dangerous combination. A woman needs to be on guard and make sure the situation is in her control."
- "Drinking makes you tired, and traveling is hard enough without that."

People had examples of stupid things they had seen people do or had done themselves when they had too much to drink.

- "Some guys got drunk and got into a car without shutting all the doors. When the driver backed up he took off one of the doors."
- "Once a male colleague and I had too much to drink, and we both tried to open the adjoining door between our rooms. I am sure we would have regretted what would

have happened. Luckily we were too drunk to figure it out or bother to go outside to the hall door."

■ "Once I drank a little too much at a firm function and fell down some stairs."

■ "At a business function a single woman went after a married man and they were kissing at the bar. They both left the company shortly after."

Don't ever feel you need to stay up late drinking or drink more than you want. Plan ahead of time what reason you will use when it is time to leave.

■ "Don't feel peer pressure to drink."

■ "Even if you go to a bar with a colleague, don't feel you need to drink more than you can handle."

■ "I leave at 10 PM and just tell people I am a morning person."

■ "If it makes you feel better, just have a ready-made excuse why you are not drinking, such as it does not react well with your allergy medicine."

■ "A guy I worked with used to say he couldn't drink and run in the morning and he preferred running."

✓ **Takeaway:** Drink moderately, if at all.

Travel Is a Time to Bond with Colleagues

Just as people are getting to know you better as you travel together, it is also an opportunity for you to get to know them. It is an excellent time to learn more about families, people's past experiences, or their ideas on business or industry issues.

One question that always comes up when you travel is whether you should break away from the group to go visit a friend in the city you are in rather than have dinner with your fellow travelers. The answer to the question is, it depends on the circumstances. If in doubt, stay with your team.

- "Having dinner with your coworkers or boss is an investment in your relationship."
- "It is nice to have dinner and reflect on what you accomplished during the day, but this does not mean you need to burn the midnight oil."
- "This is an opportunity to stay connected with people, especially if you are all from different geographic areas and do not get to see each other very often."
- "You can never miss a scheduled event."
- "If you are always trying to get away from the team, it will say something about you."
- "Generally I do not think it is a good idea to go off on your own unless there are very special circumstances such as visiting an older relative or seeing someone's new baby."
- "You should only break away if you are traveling for an extended period of time, you are not missing a team-building event, and everyone agrees you need a night off."

As more than one person pointed out, there are certain industries where travel is "chronic" and these people are constantly on the road. This group is much less likely to be offended by someone on the team getting away for a night on his or her own. How do they suggest you do this?

- "Just explain ahead of time so that everyone knows where you are going. Never be secretive or rumors will start."
- "If you want to visit a friend, keep it very loose until the last minute. You never want to say no to a client who asked you out to dinner because you made other plans."
- "If there are just two of you traveling, ask the other person how they feel about a 'night off.' Often they are relieved to have some time of their own."
- "A lot of the people in our company eat dinner in their room. After a long day, we like to catch up on email and work on other business."

Can you stay for the weekend after everyone else leaves to spend time with a friend or just visit a city you have not seen before?

- "You can stay the weekend if it is not costing your firm any money."
- "Just remember that you may have to cancel those plans if there is unexpected work coming out of the meeting."

✔ **Takeaways:** Travel is an opportunity to learn more about your colleagues and the business. Opt out of dinner only if there is a special reason and no one is insulted.

Avoid Expense Report Debacles

Never underestimate the importance of filling out your expense reports correctly and getting them done promptly. Be sure you know your company's policy on travel expenses before you even book your trip, since most companies have discounts with airlines, hotels, and rental agencies and may insist you use certain service providers. Keep all receipts, even if your fellow travelers do not bother, and write down expenses paid in cash immediately. You may think of expense reports as an administrative headache, but many managers use them as a litmus test for employees' integrity and good judgment.

- "We had an analyst who brought all his dry cleaning on a business trip, had it done at the hotel, and charged it to his room. When he expensed his hotel bill, his boss noticed the dry cleaning and rejected it. The boss didn't know what was worse: that the analyst was trying to cheat the company or he was dumb enough to think he'd get away with it."
- "Make sure you are totally honest on your expense reports. Know what is allowed and not allowed."
- "Find out who is expected to pay at meals. Companies have different cultures. At some companies the junior person pays, and at others the senior person pays."
- "Know your company's and the client's codes of con-

duct on gifts before you buy anything for a client or prospect."

✔ **Takeaways:** Fill out expense reports quickly and accurately. Know the expense policies of your company.

Random Road Warrior Rules

People have different ways of dealing with the inconveniences of business travel and are sensitive to various issues. Security was a topic raised by a number of people. When you travel, you are in unfamiliar surroundings and may be a target for criminals.

- "Make sure you focus on hotel security. Have a hotel bellhop take you to your room and check it out."
- "Be sure the desk clerk does not shout out your room number. If he does, have the room changed."
- "I never stay on the ground floor. Too easy to break in."
- "I traveled with a man who had a friend killed in a hotel fire. He always insisted we have rooms on low floors and close to fire exits."
- "As a woman I never like to eat in a restaurant alone. I usually just get room service and either work, read, or watch television."

One of the secrets to being comfortable traveling is to maintain a routine. A number of people try to build exercise into their travel schedule.

- "I am a runner, so I always take my running shoes and ask about running routes when I check in."
- "I always stay at hotels with a gym and work out early in the morning."
- "I travel with people who also like to work out, so we all go to bed at a decent hour and meet up in the gym in the

morning. It's not like we are talking on the treadmill or anything, but it's good to know we're all there working out."

Other people have different ways to make travel more comfortable.

- "I think of my room as my oasis, and I try to make travel
  as comfortable as I can. I travel with clothes I really like.
  I always have a great book to read before bed. I watch
  the same morning news show whenever I am on the road.
  Don't tell my family, but my travel routine is more relaxing than when I am at home."

Be careful about taking advantage of the hotel laundry or shoeshine.
Their schedule may not fit yours, and you could be put in an embarrassing situation if some necessary wardrobe items are missing.

- "We were staying at a hotel that had overnight shoeshine
  service, but they lost the shoes of one of my colleagues.
  Since he had only brought one pair and we had a 9:00 AM
  meeting, we had to run around and find a shoe store that
  opened early. He was not happy with the shoes he ended
  up buying."

Staying in touch with family or friends makes you feel less alone.
Try to schedule a time every day to call someone you care about,
even if just to hear a friendly voice.

- "When time differences make it necessary to call home
  during business hours, I make a call during a break. People
  don't have to know I am calling home, but I feel a lot better after I have checked in."
- "I have a ritual of faxing pictures to my kids with a
  note saying, 'I love you.' They find them very special
  and it helps when I can't call home due to different time
  zones."

What do you do with all the extra time in airports and on planes?
You can only check voice mail and email so many times.

- "Don't bother talking to the person next to you on the plane. It is a waste of your time. Don't kid yourself that it will ever lead to any business. It won't."
- "Never drink on the plane and don't hang out in bars in the airport."
- "If you are traveling during business hours it is expected that you work, either on regular work or catching up on company or industry reading."
- "On long flights, I sleep."
- "On an evening flight I feel I can read or watch a movie and not have to work the entire time."

✔ **Takeaway:** Find your own way to make travel comfortable for you, whether it is exercise, reading, or talking to family while on the road.

■ Career-Enhancing Moves

1. Learn to be a flexible business traveler who is comfortable on the road.
2. Pack lightly and carry on in an appropriate suitcase.
3. Use travel and off-site meetings as a way to build relationships with colleagues and impress senior people.

■ Career-Limiting Moves

1. Do not get drunk when traveling on business.
2. Do not damage your company's reputation by acting unprofessionally.
3. Do not cheat on your expenses.

Work and Family: You Can Manage It

The contents of this chapter are biased. If you are looking for an objective analysis of whether or not to work while you have young children, you are not going to find that discussion here. The executives interviewed for this book concluded that for them and their families, work is a very positive experience, and they highly recommended it for the people who take great pleasure in their careers. What this chapter *will* cover is how to manage work and family well so that you get the most out of both aspects of your life.

Number of Children per Executive Interviewed

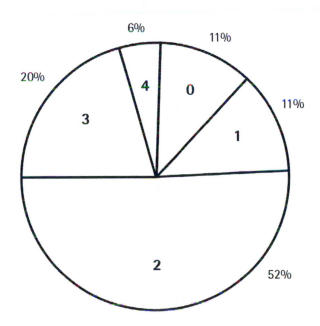

To set the stage, let me tell you a little more about the personal lives of the women interviewed. Of the 35 women, 31 had children and four did not. When I interviewed the executives, they ranged in age from 34 to 62 with an average age of 47. Only one woman had never been married, and 28, or 80 percent, were currently married. The average number of children for the group with children was 2.23, although the number of children per family ranged from one to four. Nine women had three children, and two had families of four children. Whatever stereotypes you may have of executive women, you should throw them out. They are a diverse group with the same interests and love of family as other women.

Is There a Right Time to Have Children?

While some women felt very strongly about when to have children, they did not want to tell others what to do on this emotional and highly personal subject. The women had their first child when their ages ranged from 27 to 42, and at an average age of 31. You might wonder if women are now having children later, but the youngest women interviewed had children in their early 30s. The only noticeable trend was that the women who had three to four children started having them in their late 20s to early 30s, which likely allowed them a longer time to have the family they wanted.

Some believe there is no perfect time to start a family and that it all depends on you and your spouse.

- "The right time for having kids is when your head is into it, when it is a priority and you want to make it work. Your day care will go wrong. You won't have enough money. You will have to make sacrifices. When you are willing to deal with these things, then it's the right time."
- "Your spouse has to be your partner. The two of you need to make the decision if you are going to have kids, and both of you have to make it work."
- "For me the right time to have kids was two years after I was married. I did not plan it with my career in mind."

Age of Executive at Birth of First Child

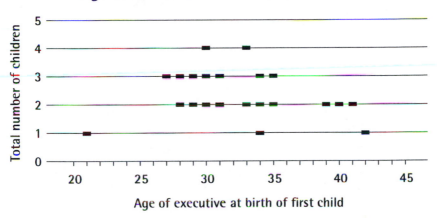

Age of executive at birth of first child

- "I don't think it matters when you have kids. Pregnancy is just a nine-month disruption in a long career."
- "I think women can be successful having babies at all ages. I am pleased they feel secure enough to do it whenever it works for them."
- "If you think about it too much, you'll think it can't be done. Just take things one at a time."
- "I hate to see women sacrifice having a family for their career. You can do both."

Some women strongly believe that earlier is better.

- "I knew children were the most important thing in my life. I wanted to have them early when I had more energy and it was easier to manage my work load."
- "The longer you wait to have children, the more ingrained you are in life without them."
- "I think it's better to have kids early. As you get older, the accountability to your job only increases. When you are at a junior level, you are able to disconnect when you go on maternity leave, and when you come back it is like nothing has happened. When I was a partner and having kids, I needed to work from home on maternity leave."

- "I think you should have kids young so you can relate to them better."

Others argued that you should not have children too early in a career.

- "If you have kids when you are too young, it can keep you from getting the foundation laid for your career. In my early years, I worked hard developing as many skills and relationships as I could. If I had had a baby then, it would have been hard to make that investment."
- "Ideally, you should be in a company at least three years before you have kids, since you will have built up some goodwill and will have more flexibility."
- "By my 30s I was more mature and organized. I knew what was important and did not panic about things. I realized that I was still my son's mother even if I was not there for everything."

A number of women mentioned the risks of believing that pregnancy could be perfectly timed for your career.

- "Don't wait too long to have children. No one wants to admit there are fertility curves, which I never appreciated until I tried to have kids. It turned out I had both of my kids by in vitro fertilization. Having children is not something you can do at any point you want."
- "You can't always control the timing. I had several miscarriages. Don't wait until life is all figured out. This is a life decision, and you cannot revisit it."
- "I spent seven years doing in vitro fertilization."
- "I worry that people will wait until it is too late. I would not have put having kids in jeopardy. At the end of the day your family is your family and your job is your job."
- "The mistake I have seen is women waiting too long."

However, some women who waited longer to have children were happy that they did.

- "I don't recommend having children between 25 and 35, which are the partnership-making years. I was willing to take a roll of the dice, understanding I might not be able to have children, but I really wanted to have a successful career."
- "I wanted to be a partner before I had children. I wanted to be sure I had a clean shot at it. I was prepared that if I couldn't have a child, I would adopt. I knew I would be a parent at some point."
- "It is easier the higher you are in a company. You have more flexibility and you are not under a microscope. You have already proved yourself and have credibility."
- "I was not comfortable about doing it earlier. Having a child while I was proving myself would have been too much for me."

Are there any really bad times to consider having children?

- "I can't imagine having kids while going through professional school."
- "Having three in a row and taking six months off each time is very difficult. That means there will be a long stretch when you are not there, and it will be hard to develop relationships."
- "The wrong time to have kids is when you and your spouse are not comfortable with the fact that having a child will change how you spend your time."

✔ **Takeaways:** Start a family when you and your spouse are ready for the changes a child will bring to your lifestyle. Some argue that younger mothers have more flexibility at work and fewer fertility problems. Others recommend having children later so that you can concentrate on getting your career firmly on track before becoming a parent.

Planning Maternity Leave and Going Back to Work

The amount of time women took off to have their children varied greatly—from two weeks to two years. Women tended to take off the same amount for each child, although it was not clear if this reflected their own desires or the policies of their employers. The most common maternity leave was three months.

- "Don't worry about taking time off. When you come back it will be like you never left. You don't get a badge of honor for coming back early, so take your time."
- "Wait to tell people at the office that you are pregnant until after the first trimester when the risk of miscarriage is lower. However, if you are sick all the time you may be forced to tell at least your boss earlier."

There was not always a "switch" from full-time maternity leave to full-time work.

- "I took eight weeks of official maternity leave and worked another eight weeks with a short work week of four days a week."

Age of Executive at Birth of First Child

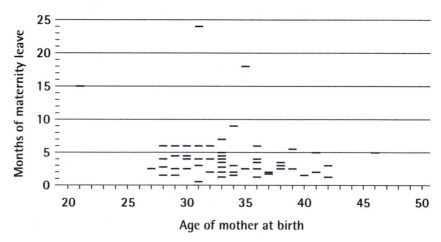

- "I nursed the first child for 11 months and the second child for 15 months, and went home during lunch to nurse. When I traveled I pumped breast milk."
- "I waited until my son was six months old before I did any overnight travel."

Remember that life went on at the company while you were gone and that there may be some tension when you return.

- "If people covered for you while you were out, acknowledge that and thank them. Offer to cover for them if they ever need it."
- "When I came back from maternity leave, the person reporting to me who had been covering my accounts made it very clear he thought he should just keep my accounts and he resenting having me back."
- "Everyone is working one and a half jobs already these days, so when one person is out it can be overwhelming to other people."

Don't expect to just resume life as normal. People may be watching to see if you are as dedicated as you were before having a child. It is not personal. Bosses have just seen too many successful women leave the workforce to assume you will stay. Once you have decided that you want to stay, you should make it known that you are glad to be back.

- "You do not know how important a career is going to be to someone once they have a baby. Sometimes the people you thought were very career-focused decide to stay at home, and others you thought were not as committed sail right through."
- "I work for a family-friendly company but they are so ready to accommodate me and encourage me to take time off that I am worried I am going to be accommodated right off the fast track."

✔ **Takeaways:** Maternity leave for this group was most commonly three months. When you return from leave, thank the people who covered for you. You may need to prove that you are as committed to your career as you were before you had a child.

Child Care Must Provide Flexibility for the Parents

Child care arrangements need to match the work needs of both parents. Different jobs have different work hours, travel requirements, and commutes, so the choice of child care should reflect the parents' needs as much as the child's. There is also the question of availability of child care, which varies between the cities and the suburbs. The families had child care that ranged from day care to full-time live-in help, and child care arrangements changed over time as children got older.

- "Our child care has shifted as the kids grew and their needs changed. We have always had a live-out nanny who was very nurturing, but we started having a second person come in, a college student, to help with homework in the afternoons."
- "I had au pairs for many years, but as the kids got older I switched to a housekeeper who could take care of the household logistics and drive."
- "It took me a while to realize the babysitter could do more than just take care of the kids. I had her do the grocery shopping, dry cleaning, and any other errands. That way when I came home I could just spend time with my children. I didn't hire a sitter, I hired a wife. Every working mother needs one."
- "I've always had a full-time live-in from Monday at 7 AM to Friday at 7 PM, and it has made all the difference in the world. I don't think you can be in a professional services job and deal with child care not showing up."
- "We have a rule that we need to have at least two adults in the house during the critical homework/dinner/bathing hours, so even though we have a full-time live-in, we have a college student come from 4 to 8 PM."

- "I have a nanny for 12 hours a day. I wanted one caregiver with a parenting style similar to mine. My husband leaves later in the morning, and I am home earlier in the evening."
- "I use corporate child care close to the office for the youngest, and my older child is in a private school close to where I work, so I can get to either one if there is a problem."
- "I have a long commute, so I have a full-time live-in. I needed that stability."

Many people said that good child care was one of the best investments parents will ever make.

- "You need good child care where you do not have to worry about your kids during the day. The commute home is when you mentally start to shift back to your family."
- "Get the best child care you can afford. We have always paid more than the market rate, and it has been worth it."
- "You need to think like a businessperson in managing your family as well. The only way you can do everything is to spend money for good child care and housekeeping. Think of it as the cost of doing business."

It is not just child care you need to think about, it is all the services that can make your life easier. If you can afford it, hire people to do the things you do not enjoy so that you can spend more time with your family.

- "It is a balancing act to be a working parent. The key is good help."
- "It is difficult to do everything well. Outsource as much as possible."
- "Overinvest in help at home."
- "Don't skimp on services. We have a sitter, a housekeeper, someone to do yard work, a plow guy, and the dry cleaning picked up and delivered."
- "Once my kids were older and we no longer had a sitter to cook meals, I felt pressured to rush home and cook, which I hated. I found a chef who filled our refrigerator with fully prepared meals we just had to heat up."

The type of child care you have is one of those things that employers are not supposed to ask about but are very interested in knowing. The question is whether the employee will be able to do her job at the level expected.

- "The type of help a woman chooses tells me how seriously she takes her career. If she has an older woman five days a week who can cover if she is late, that will work. If she has a 40-hour-a-week au pair, that doesn't even cover regular work hours and getting to and from the office. When someone tells me she has an au pair, I know that will not work in this job."
- "It is a problem when I see someone with no backup in the family's child care. If you have three kids and keep them in a day care center and have no alternative when they get sick, that will not work since that happens often. If you have a good job and you want to keep it, you better have a plan for normal things like sick kids and occasionally staying late."
- "Many women do reveal too much about themselves, but in many cases they need to do so to assure the boss or client that they can manage work and family. However, be careful that you disclose enough to give them confidence that the work will get done, but do not go into the gory details of the juggling you are doing."
- "Some women say they need to leave at 4:30 PM for the train no matter what else is going on, and it drives the rest of us crazy."

✔ **Takeaways:** Invest in good child care that will allow you to focus on your job. Outsource as many services as you can. Tell your boss about your child care arrangements to pre-empt any concerns.

Support Starts at Home

One message came across loud and clear: the key to successfully balancing work and family was picking the right spouse. The general conclusion was that you could manage with a supportive spouse or even on your own if you had to, but an unsupportive spouse made life impossible. So, if you are not married yet, read the suggestions below very carefully.

- "My husband has been unbelievable. Many times I said I wanted to quit, and he said that staying home would not be good for me."
- "Repeat this mantra: marry well. By that I mean find someone who is supportive and will propel you in your career."
- "Marry your best friend. You can't do it without a supportive husband. Mine has always been there, and he is my biggest fan. A bad spouse would be someone who robbed you of your self."
- "If you have a solid marriage, then things are much easier."
- "You can't do it married to an unsupportive husband. You don't want a husband who adds to your stress."
- "Strong women need even stronger men; find one who can support you, appreciate you, and see you as a life partner."
- "My husband was traveling two weeks a month when we had our child, but we arranged never to be traveling at the same time."

That is not to say that these women found perfect husbands—they just figured out a way to deal with the stresses in normal family life.

- "That does not mean we don't argue. We do, but since he believes in me, our kids are OK with everything."
- "Having young kids is the most stressful time in your marriage. We never got close to divorce, but there were some very difficult times."
- "There is stress in the equation, but we think it has been worth it in the end."

The other suggestion was to talk to your kids and be sure they understand that they are part of a working family unit. Working mothers felt it was good for their children to appreciate work from an early age.

- "I come from an immigrant family, and all the women I met worked. The kids knew the families were all working to do the best they could for the family and that the kids were part of the team."
- "You need to communicate to your kids that you feel good about working."
- "You need a great support network. My husband was great, our sitter was great, and we expected our kids to do more."
- "I feel so good about what I do every day that it is good for my kids to see."
- "Not only was my husband supportive of my working but so were my kids. They thought it was cool. My son said he'd like a working wife since then he would not feel so responsible for everything."

✔ **Takeaways:** You need a supportive spouse to balance work and family, so marry well. Talk to your children about work and help them feel part of the team.

Coworkers Are Not Your Regular Backup

One of the keys to moving ahead in your career after having a child is to make balancing work and family look easy. Parents know that managing all the demands on their time is difficult, but coworkers do not need to hear all your problems. While they may cover for you in a true crisis, no one wants to work with someone who has constant crises.

- "It is tough to manage work and family, but don't expect the firm to manage it for you. You need to decide what it is going to take to get it done and make it work."
- "Keep your stress out of the workplace, or people will ques-

tion your commitment. Don't make it difficult for others. I have seen this hurt women's careers."

- "Most people are very accommodating of other people's schedules, but there needs to be fair play. If a person is taking time off, she needs to make up the time so that she is not imposing on the rest of the group. People with children do end up taking more time off, but most of the time it works out. I still expect them to get the job done."
- "I like to be supportive of family issues when I can, but it is a business relationship and you are paying someone to get a job done. In the short term people at work can help out, but in the long run the employee needs to make it work."
- "People are usually very good about pitching in when there is an adoption or birth, an issue with elder parents, an illness, or anything viewed as short term. The problem comes when people have situations that are not considered serious, such as where someone with little kids has constant child care crises. That looks long term and people resent covering."
- "Some people are always drama kings or queens. You need to be able to handle things in an organized way. If you use up your goodwill, people will not cut you a lot of slack."

✔ **Takeaways:** Your coworkers do not want to hear about the stresses of balancing work and family. Do not ask for backup often or you will alienate people.

Forget the Guilt

Do working mothers feel guilty? Sometimes yes, most times no. Every parent wishes he or she could spend more time with his or her children, but everyone knows it is a balancing act and you do the best you can. Even parents who are at home are often busy with other children, elder parents, or charitable activities and not able to always be there for the children.

- "Never feel guilty. You are not going to be able to do everything, but schedule important events for your children on your business calendar and treat those like critical appointments."
- "Sometimes my daughter tries to lay on the guilt that I am not a stay-at-home mom. I may not be picking my kids up from school, but I go to their games and important events."
- "I am a better mother because I am happy with myself."
- "I rationalize that my children are better off that I work, since I am more personally satisfied."
- "The only guilt I have is that I do not feel guilty."
- "Decide what is right for you and accept the consequences. You must live with your decisions."
- "I made the big events and skipped the class picnics and parent coffees, and my son complained I was never at school. When I was between jobs I started going to everything, and then he complained I was at school too much. You can't win with kids."
- "Women have self-imposed stress. You are not the only parent who can go to a school meeting and bring cookies to the bake sale."

Certain women do feel guilty about certain aspects of their life.

- "I feel guilty that my husband bears the emotional burden of the kids during the week, since I get home later than he does at night and I often travel. It is not always pleasant dealing with kids, and I know it can be stressful for him."
- "One time I missed a school play because of plane problems, and I felt so guilty."
- "I hate not being there when it is time for my kids to go to bed."
- "I feel guilty about everything. It is just in my makeup. When I am at work I feel guilty about home, and when I am at home I feel guilty about work."

While few women struggled with guilt about balancing work and family, they had some regrets.

- "It was harder when the kids were little and I was missing out on their 'firsts.' Periodically, I feel bad about the long hours, but it is clear in my mind what my priorities are, and when I need to be there, I am."
- "I regret I have never taken my kids on a class field trip."
- "I regret not having more time at home, but that is just for my own selfish reasons."
- "I regret I do not take better care of myself."
- "I missed my friend's wedding for work, and I have always regretted it."

My favorite conversation about regret was with a woman who said she regretted that her sons were not as well informed about the news as she would like and she felt this was a failing as a mother. When I asked her how the family spent its time, she said they were all into sports and were either at someone's game or talking about sports. I laughed because my own kids grew up reading three newspapers every day and both have *The New York Times* as their home page, but they complain that I did not teach them enough about sports. I guess no parent is perfect, and we all pass on our own passions to our kids.

Just as you should not feel guilty about going to work, you should also not feel guilty—or feel the need to explain yourself—when you leave the office for a family commitment.

- "If you have to leave, just say 'I have another commitment.' Don't apologize."
- "If you commit to attending an event or performance, do not miss it unless it is totally unavoidable. Underpromise and then exceed their expectations."

✔ **Takeaways:** Don't feel guilty about working. You can't do everything, but arrange your schedule to attend major events at your children's school, such as concerts, important games, and teacher conferences.

Part-Time Work May Not Derail Careers

I only specifically chose one woman whom I knew had worked part-time, but discovered that seven out of the 35 women interviewed, or 20 percent, had worked part-time for long periods of time and two women continue to do this. Despite concerns about never getting back on track, all of these women achieved senior positions, and two were specifically asked to move from part-time to full-time to assume leadership positions in their firms.

- "I worked four days a week for two years. After my second child was born, I went back to work five days a week and it was easier. I just could not do my job well with young kids at home."
- "For 10 years I worked part-time, which at our firm means 35–40 hours per week rather than 80 hours per week. I was paid 60 percent of normal pay and was available for my clients at their discretion."
- "When I came back it was for three days a week. A year after becoming a partner, I ran a business unit while I was part-time."
- "I worked four days per week at 80 percent pay."

The keys to a successful part-time arrangement seemed to be picking the right company and being flexible about the hours put in and days you work. Women at both professional service firms and traditional corporations had successfully managed part-time work.

- "You need a company willing to make it possible, and you need to make it work. You need to be at a place where part-timers are not second-class citizens."
- "I have people working for me part-time and they are wonderful contributors. A successful 'special relationship' depends on a strong foundation of trust between the employee and supervisor. It is difficult to create that trust with a new person, so you need to have an existing relationship before you ask for any unusual arrangement."
- "I see women trying to work part-time, and it is very hard in today's environment. Some companies are willing to do

it and some are not. It is more acceptable for some jobs than others."

- "Yes, I would do it again. It did not slow my career to partner, but I was careful whom I worked for."
- "I work four days a week and take Wednesday off. However, it is rare that I don't do some work from home that day."
- "You need to be flexible what days you work in a professional firm. Saying you work Monday/Tuesday/Thursday won't work. You need to be on call."
- "You need to be flexible and decide if it is the right time to say 'That meeting is on the day I take off. Can we reschedule?'"

One executive encouraged part-time work rather than leaving after having a child.

- "Don't think you can step outside the workforce for five to six years and come back at the same level. Work part-time if you can't manage full-time."

There are some downsides to working part-time, and it is not for everyone. The general feeling is you work more hours than you get credit for and you are not paid for the extra time.

- "I think it is harder to work part-time, since you feel divided. It's easier to just go to work every day."
- "I stepped off the career path and worked part-time for a few years, but I felt I had a foot in two worlds and was not doing well in either. My career was not moving upward and I was not meant to be a stay-at-home mom. Those were my guilty years. I went back full-time and felt better."
- "A part-time worker will always be a little bit exploited. If you say you are going to work 75 percent time, you will likely end up working at least 80 percent."

✔ Takeaways: Pick the right firm and the right job if you want to work part-time. Be flexible about hours and days worked to get the job done.

Balance Is Key to Managing Stress

You can't spend all your time working and taking care of a family. Well, you can, but it is not a good idea. The executives found that other activities—either with their families or alone—were great stress relievers and helped them put work in perspective. It also makes you a more interesting person and gives you things to talk about with colleagues and clients.

- "You need balance in your life and to have activities outside of work. Kids provide some of that balance, but you need to do some things for yourself."
- "You need to find time for things you enjoy."
- "It is important to have a hobby away from work."

Many women were into sports, and they often shared activities they enjoyed with family and friends.

- "My husband and I run together every day."
- "I run three and a half miles after work. When the kids were younger they would get on their bikes and act as my pace car and tell me about their days."
- "Golf is great, since you can play it any time by yourself. I also have played tennis, although there were some gap years when the kids were young."
- "The gym is important for stress relief, but I am most inclined to skip it during the times I need it most."
- "I cross-country ski in the winter and hike during the summer."
- "I do Pilates, yoga, and running. I used to do it five days a week, but now it's two to three days. I arrange to meet friends at the gym so I can exercise and see them at the same time."
- "As a family we go hiking and camping."
- "The weekend is family time, and in the winter that means skiing."
- "In the summer it is golf and biking, and in the winter it's skiing."

The arts and entertainment were popular, and this is an area where many women had taken leadership positions, fulfilling the "do good while having fun" role discussed in the networking section. Charities of various kinds also benefited from these women's time.

- "I love the ballet and am head of the finance committee of our city ballet company."
- "We are members of all the museums. I do lecture series with my husband. I take an art class with my sister to stay connected. I have done glassblowing. Now that the kids are older we take them to the museums as well."
- "I am involved in a lot of charitable organizations. I have to shift gears, but need something with enough intellectual challenge to drive work out of my mind."
- "I am involved in a lot of community service organizations, and I bring my son with me to meetings. I just incorporated him into my other activities."

Many of the women were on boards of directors or committees of their children's schools. This seemed to be a great way to stay in touch with their children's lives, do some networking, and give back.

Other women had hobbies that you might not associate with high-powered executives.

- "I quilt. I started when my kids were in high school, and I have made one for each child."
- "I have written three novels. I needed something for myself, and it was a way of reclaiming some personal space."
- "I sew, which I find very therapeutic, and give crafts as gifts. My aunt was a seamstress who lived with us and taught us all how to sew, and I passed this on to my kids."
- "I belong to a gourmet food club. In this city, eating is a hobby."
- "I love architecture and fine arts, and I redecorate our house every five years or so."

You do not have to have an official hobby. There are many ways to relax with and without your family.

- "I am an extrovert, so when I want to recharge my batteries, I go out and see people. A friend of mine is an introvert, and she reads or meditates."
- "I get together with friends and classmates, and I am trying to keep a journal."
- "I love movies and walking my dog."
- "I find gardening very relaxing."
- "I am a lessonaholic. I take guitar lessons, have a trainer, and have taken French lessons."
- "All of my free time revolves around my family. My husband and I have both been coaches. I have been a Girl Scout leader and a religious studies teacher."
- "The week is all work, but the weekend is not. We spend Saturdays in the temple, which is our social community."
- "I teach Sunday school and have joined the church choir."
- "I am active in our church youth ministry."

✔ **Takeaways:** Find activities you enjoy to relieve the stresses of work and family. Not only will you have fun, you also will become a more interesting person.

Notes from the Front Lines

Every family manages things a little differently, but there is some general advice women wanted to pass on to those considering how to "do it all." Some of the advice focused on finding the right company, which is often referred to as family-friendly, but really means finding a company and job that fit your needs.

- "Go to the right employer before you have kids. Some will be very supportive and others will make you sneak around if you need to take time off. Are they looking at you as a body or a future partner?"
- "You need to be realistic about what job you have when

you have kids. You may not want to be in a position that requires you to be in Europe for two weeks a month."

- "Ask yourself if you are at a firm where you can work in less than fifth gear."
- "Go into a job where you can be an equal in power and money but that does not require you to do a lot of weekend work. For example, at an investment banking firm you might be better off on the trading floor than in the investment banking department."
- "There is a high opportunity cost to being away from your children, so you need to be happy at work to make it all worthwhile."
- "Ask other women at your company, off the record, how they made it work. By the time you talk to your supervisor you should be presenting solutions, not problems. A lot of what you can do depends on how you are viewed."
- "If it is just too much, you need to change something. You can't change your kids, so you need to change your job."

You also need to set realistic expectations for yourself and your family. Mark this section and reread it whenever you feel like inadequate parent or you are not moving fast enough in your career.

- "You have to accept the fact that you can never make everyone happy all the time. I have three constituencies, work, kids and spouse, and there are times when someone will be unhappy."
- "When you have kids you need to develop a new scorecard, because you are in a new game. The old game was based on how fast you got promoted. To be successful in the new game you need to slow down and understand the richness of your life. Develop a clear picture of what success means and set new career and home goals."
- "Remember this is a marathon and not a sprint. I got promoted four months later than my peers, but that is OK in the long run."
- "Don't be a perfectionist. It is unrealistic to think you can have a fabulous home, kids out of a catalogue, and do a

lot of entertaining. Don't expect to be Martha Stewart. Have realistic expectations of your children as well as yourself. Focus on what is important to you."

- "I know I am probably not the best mother all the time and I am probably not the best professional all the time, but I am very good at both."
- "You can't be supermom. You can have it all, but not all of everything."
- "Don't be too hard on yourself or set your expectations too high. Focus your attention where it is needed. If you have happy, healthy kids, then things are OK at home, but if things are off balance, you need a little more attention on the home front and your career may need to slow down a little."
- "You need to keep the big picture in mind. If you are devoting more of yourself to the job than is necessary, you must remember not to sacrifice your personal life for your job. If something is important at home, then do it."

There are also some good ideas for how to stay connected. Children don't need you there every minute.

- "I take my kids to the bus stop every morning."
- "Stay with the moment you are in. Kids notice if you are checking your Blackberry or talking on the cell phone at the soccer game."
- "You can mother by phone. Email and IM make it even easier. Just because you are not face-to-face does not mean you cannot talk. I've had some great conversations from the London airport."
- "You can be affectionate in different ways. I have left presents for my kids under their beds when I am traveling."
- "I always stay in touch if I have to work on a weekend."

✔ **Takeaways:** Pick the right company before you have children. Set realistic expectations for your home life and career.

So, How Are the Kids?

Every single person said she would quit work if she thought it were having an adverse effect on her children—but none had. So, how have the children fared with working mothers? In our sample, the "children" ranged from babies to two mothers themselves.

- "I have three well-adjusted, happy kids. They have had unconditional love, which is the most important thing in life."
- "My daughters are very independent. We raised them in a household where they were very engaged and understood our decisions, and now they are making great ones on their own."
- "My daughter told me she went to a recruiting session on campus where some students were aggressively questioning a working mother about how she could travel and have kids, and the woman was quite shaken at the criticism of her parenting skills. At the end of the session my daughter went up to her and said, 'My mother had the same job as yours at another company, and my brother and I turned out great.' The woman smiled and thanked her."
- "My daughter is so independent and well adjusted that when she went off to college, she had no problems. She calls to talk, but every so often I wish she'd cry on my shoulder. Sometimes I think she does not need me."
- "My daughter sees other mothers managing their kids like a deal, and she tells me she is happy that I am not micro-managing her life."

✔ **Takeaway:** The children of working mothers are just as likely to be happy and well adjusted as other children.

■ Career-Enhancing Moves

1. Marry a spouse who supports your desire to work.
2. Have good child care arrangements that are flexible enough to allow you to stay late or travel when necessary.
3. Do something in your life to balance the stress, whether it is taking up a hobby, sports, reading, or religious activities.

■ Career-Limiting Moves

1. Do not complain about the daily stresses of managing a job and family at your work.
2. Do not ask coworkers to cover for you except in an extreme emergency.

Ten

Where Do You Go from Here?

We have talked about many different issues, but how do they apply to you and your career? Right now you are doing one of the best things you can do for your career—stepping back and reflecting on it.

Just as a chief executive officer needs to think strategically about her business, you need to think strategically about your career. I have told many CEOs that the problem with creating a strategic plan is not that the management team lacks the knowledge to build a great plan designed specifically for that company. The problem is these managers are just too busy "making the numbers" this week, this month, this quarter, to ever raise their heads and look farther out. Many companies rush through a "budget" once a year and call it a "strategic plan," but the result is just a summation of spreadsheets provided by the business units, and the plan does not truly reflect the vision for the business held by the management team.

Hardworking people have the same problem doing career planning. You are probably so busy with your job that you never carve out the time to consider your own career needs. If you are like many people, you only seriously think about your career once a year when you are required to do a formal review for your company. Given that that review is often used for compensation purposes, you should put yourself in the best light and not list all the improvements you need to make. Besides, many of the skills you want to acquire may not be available in your current company, and you certainly should not focus on anything in your review that implies you are not a loyal employee who is fully dedicated to the firm. Therefore, if you want a strategic career plan that accounts for all of your professional and personal needs, it should be done separately from your formal company review.

Think of the issues that a review written *by you for you* should consider. Ask yourself the following questions and write down your answers.

- What do you want to be doing in three years, five years, 10 years?
- What skills will you need to do those jobs well?
- If you do not have those skills, can you get them in your current job or elsewhere in the company where you work now? Do you need to go somewhere else?
- If you can acquire those skills in your company but need to be in a different department, how can you transfer there?
- If you need to change companies to achieve your goals, where do you want to go and what is the best way of getting hired there?
- Do you have the right educational background to be a top contender for the positions you want to hold? If not, what degree(s) do you need and how soon can you start working toward them?
- How much money do you want to make, both now and over the long term?
- How many hours per week are you willing to put in year after year to make that money? Are you willing to work nights and weekends often or just occasionally?
- Do you enjoy traveling and, if so, how many days a month?
- What family plans do you have and how will they fit into your career plans? Are there other family considerations, such as the desire to be close to parents, siblings, or extended family?
- What other personal needs do you have that should be worked into your career goals? These may include time for religious, sports, charitable, or cultural activities.

Now you should understand why the "review" at work is not career planning at all. Who is going to tell her boss that she will never consider an overseas assignment because she wants to see her nieces and nephews grow up? Maybe you will, but, if so, you are braver than most people.

What if you do not know exactly what you want to do in 10, five, or even three years? Such uncertainty is extremely common, so don't get nervous. Ask yourself these questions:

- Do you like to work in groups, or do you prefer to work alone?
- Do you like knowing what you are going to do when you go to work every day or do you enjoy constant change?
- Do you like to be in one place, whether this is an office, lab, or factory, or do you enjoy traveling from client to client?
- What are you good at, and where have you been successful in the past?

You know a lot more about yourself than you think. Once you decide what keeps you motivated and the work environment you prefer, consider jobs that incorporate these things. If you are not sure, talk to mentors, people in your network, or family friends. These people should preferably be outside your company so that you can be completely honest.

How often should you consider your career plan and make corrections? Think of career planning the same way experts advise that you manage your money: do a detailed review once a year and a quick checkup quarterly. You do not need to look at your career weekly or monthly unless you have a problem. Financial advisers tell you that when you manage your money you should consider the level of risk you are comfortable with over the long term and the expected returns of the different asset classes, such as stocks, bonds, and cash, in light of changing circumstances. When one asset class gets too large you should rebalance, or move assets, to better reflect the risk you are willing to take to achieve your long-term financial objectives. Your career is very similar in that you may decide your career "portfolio" (or résumé) now has too much of one type of skill to achieve your long-term career objectives and it is time to rebalance your skills by changing jobs or companies to achieve your career goals.

When you do your career planning, remember that we live in a constantly changing world. Be sure you develop skills that are broad enough that they can be used in different positions by many companies. Be sure you can communicate effectively, both verbally and in written form, even if you were a math or science major. Remain current on standard technologies, even if you were an English major. Your job may disappear through downsizing, merger, or outsourcing, and your career plan may go off track. Learn to be flexible and adapt.

One last point to remember: all you have is your time, and there is never enough of it. You spend a lot of that time with the people at work, so you need to enjoy being with them. You don't need to love them, or even like them every day, but if you do not wake up excited to go to work nine days out of 10, you are in the wrong place. I am a firm believer that there is a right company for everyone. If you hate where you are, don't blame the company, just find another place where you fit in. Companies have distinct cultures, so be sure you meet enough people in the interview process to understand that culture and whether you will enjoy working there.

The 35 women who shared their careers with me so that I could write this book all enjoy working. They believe, as I do, that work is one of the most rewarding experiences we will ever have. These women and I are reaching out to you, the next generation, through this book, not just so that you can go further and faster than we did, but so that you can enjoy life more in the process. We want you to know that success and a good family life are very compatible. Hard work and having fun can go hand in hand. Achievements are even better when shared with colleagues and friends.

Life is like a marathon. There are certain milestones where the crowd cheers for you, and there are lonely stretches where you are tired and alone, but you need to keep moving and stay on your pace. It's your life and your career, so go out there and run the race you want to run.

Index

To order additional copies of *What You Don't Know and Your Boss Won't Tell You*

Web: www.itascabooks.com

Phone: 1-800-901-3480

Fax: Copy and fill out the form below with credit card information. Fax to 763-398-0198.

Mail: Copy and fill out the form below. Mail with check or credit card information to:

Syren Book Company
5120 Cedar Lake Road
Minneapolis, MN 55416

Order Form

Copies	Title / Author	Price	Totals
	***What You Don't Know and Your Boss Won't Tell You* / Pamela F. Lenehan**	$15.95	$
	Subtotal		$
	7% sales tax (MN only)		$
	Shipping and handling, first copy		$ 4.00
	Shipping and handling, ___ add'l copies @ $1.00 ea.		$
	TOTAL TO REMIT		$

Payment Information:

__ Check Enclosed __ Visa/MasterCard	
Card number:	Expiration date:
Name on card:	
Billing address:	
City:	State: Zip:
Signature:	Date:

Shipping Information:

__ Same as billing address __ Other (enter below)	
Name:	
Address:	
City:	State: Zip: